INTERVIEWING

Annette Garrett

Interviewing

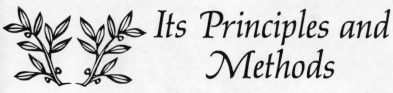 *Its Principles and Methods*

ELINOR P. ZAKI AND MARGARET M. MANGOLD

FAMILY SERVICE ASSOCIATION OF AMERICA
NEW YORK

International Standard Book Number: 0-87304-097-X (paper)
International Standard Book Number: 0-87304-098-8 (cloth)
Library of Congress Catalog Card Number: 72-78003

Printed in the United States of America

Designed by Joan Stoliar

4 5 6 7 8 9 10

 3

Foreword

The Family Service Association of America first published *Interviewing: Its Principles and Methods* by Annette Garrett in 1942. Miss Garrett was Associate Director of Smith College School for Social Work from 1934 until her death in 1957.

The book was written in response to numerous requests that the Association had received for in-service training material for new agencies and established agencies that were expanding their services. The response to *Interviewing* was an immediately enthusiastic one. Even so, the Association did not anticipate that within a few years the book would become the basic text for teaching interviewing, not only to social workers, but also to nurses, teachers, physicians, psychologists, volunteers in community activities, and personnel in industry.

Because of the continued demand for it, the book, with no revision, has been kept in print for thirty years and has had thirty-one printings. *Interviewing* has attained the status of a true classic in social work literature, and almost a quarter of a million copies in English have been sold. Its international reputation is attested to by the fact that it has been translated into nineteen foreign languages, from Arabic to Urdu! It is available in Braille and on phonograph records produced in the United States and abroad.

Requests for a revised edition have increased in recent years. Inevitably the requestors pointed out that the principles outlined by Miss Garrett remain as valid as when they were written and that it was the case illustrations that needed to be replaced by contemporary examples. The editors, in deciding to revise the book, agreed that Miss Garrett's depth of understanding of people and sensitivity to the feelings that underlie spoken words are indeed timeless. It is our hope that the addition of interviews illustrative of current practice, combined with Miss Garrett's simple, clearly written yet profound statements of principles, will be helpful to persons engaged in interviewing in a variety of situations and settings.

It has been particularly pleasant and satisfying for me to work again with Elinor P. Zaki, former Director of Publications Service of FSAA and now Director of Community Relations of the Family Service Association of Greater Boston. We are greatly indebted to several colleagues for their interest and consultative help in the selection of the new illustrative interviews:

Celia Benney, Associate Executive Director, Altro Health and Rehabilitation Services, New York;

Anne Ford, Director of Professional Services, Family Service Association of Greater Boston;

Mary K. Keeley, Director of Staff Development, Travelers Aid–International Social Service of America, New York;

Elizabeth Robichaud, Director of Services, Travelers Aid Society of New York;

Alice Rogers, Assistant Director of Social Service, Massachusetts General Hospital, Boston; and

Nancy Staver, Chief of Psychiatric Social Work, Judge Baker Guidance Center, Boston.

I also wish to express our warm appreciation to Marcia Kovarsky of the Publications Service staff for her expert assistance as copy and production editor of the second edition of *Interviewing*.

MARGARET M. MANGOLD
Director, Publications Service
Family Service Association
of America

April, 1972

Contents

PART ONE *The Nature of Interviewing*

PART TWO *Illustrative Interviews*

PART ONE *The Nature of Interviewing*

1 Interviewing as an Art

Everyone engages in interviewing. Sometimes he interviews; sometimes he is interviewed. The mother interviews the principal of the school in which she is thinking of entering her son. The principal, in turn, interviews the mother and the boy. A young man is interviewed by his prospective employer and, in turn, interviews the employer. Some people, because of the nature of their work, spend a good deal of time in interviewing. The attendant in an information booth devotes all his working hours to miniature interviews. Lawyers, doctors, nurses, newspapermen, policemen, ministers, counselors, credit men, personnel managers, employers, all devote a considerable amount of time to talking with people, getting information from them, advising them, helping them. They acquire various degrees of skill in the art of interviewing, sometimes consciously, usually unconsciously. One group who are interviewers par excellence are social caseworkers. Their tasks make them professional interviewers, and for some of them interviewing becomes an art and, indeed, almost a science, some of whose basic principles at least they are able to formulate and organize into the beginnings of a systematic body of knowledge.

Probably everyone starting to interview wishes there was a list of rules he could follow. Unfortunately, however, it is impossible to enumerate a complete list of infallible rules for all interviewing, or even for any particular kind. Interviewing takes place between human beings, and people are too individual to be reduced to a formula. To be sure, there are certain psychological traits that characterize most people most of the time, and a skilled interviewer will do well to keep some of the more important ones in mind. There are characteristic modes of human action and reaction, and awareness of them tends to increase the satisfactoriness of one's relationship with others. Interviewing involves a closer and subtler relation between human beings than may at first be recognized, and skill in conducting this relationship can be increased through knowledge of the fundamental factors involved.

Some people fear that a self-conscious study of the principles of interviewing may detract from the warm friendliness and real interest in other individuals that are so essential for the successful practice of the art. There is certainly no necessity for warmth and friendliness to disappear with knowledge. An informed person need not be unfriendly. One need not be ignorant of human psychology to love human beings. Indeed, the opposite is often true. There are few things so frustrating as to love someone but not know how to give the help he desperately needs; contrariwise, to be able to help those we love increases our affection for them.

Warm human interest does sometimes vanish from interviewing, and when that happens it becomes a monotonous, mechanical sort of thing that is relatively valueless. But the cause of this kind of interviewing, when it occurs, is not knowledge of the rich interplay of one human mind with another, but the ignorance that regards interviewing as a routine affair of asking set questions and recording answers. Interviewing is indeed far more than a routine procedure. With a proper understanding of even some of the intricacies of human personality and of the effective give-and-take between two complex human beings, our attention and warm interest are aroused in increasing measure, and the interviewing process becomes anything but routine.

Interviewing is an art, a skilled technique that can be improved and eventually perfected primarily through continued practice. But mere practice alone is not enough. Skills can be developed to their fullest only when practice is accompanied by knowledge about interviewing and conscious study of one's own practice. Knowledge of the theory underlying interviewing gives us certain material in the light of which we can critically examine our present techniques and discern ways in which they can be improved.

The obvious fact about interviewing is that it involves communication between two people. It might be called professional conversation. Special problems confront both interviewer and interviewee. We begin to obtain some notion of the complexities involved if we recall some of the feelings we ourselves have had while on the way to be interviewed. Perhaps we were seeking to borrow money, were consulting a doctor or a lawyer, or were applying for a job. We may have felt some fear at the prospect of talking with an unknown person and of revealing our needs to him. We may have been uncertain as to just what about ourselves we might have to tell, fearful that the interviewer might wish to know more than we were willing to relate, might not understand us, or might not grant our request.

On the other hand, when we first began to interview, what were some of the worries that plagued us? We wondered whether we would say the right things to put our client at his ease. Would we be able to draw him out? What would we do if he did not talk, and if he did, would we be sure to recognize and select the significant facts in his remarks and behavior?

For an interview to be successful, the diverse fears of both interviewer and interviewee must be allayed, and the diverse desires of both must be met. Rapport must be established between the two, a relationship that will enable the interviewee to reveal the essential facts of his situation and that will enable the interviewer to be most effective in helping him.

To give meaning and background to the suggestions for interviewing that we make later and to enable the interviewer to carry out these suggestions with understanding, we shall devote the next chapter to a study of certain basic facts about human nature, concentrating our attention on those that are most significant for interviewing. The following comments indicate the special areas that will be discussed in some detail.

Although most of us feel the need at times for expert legal or medical knowledge, we tend to feel that we already possess an adequate working knowledge of the nature of human beings and their behavior. But such knowledge is likely to be a combination of old wives' tales and generalizations based on our own necessarily limited experience and distorted by our own peculiar blind spots. We interpret others in relation to ourselves, forgetting that our own view is influenced by a host of more or less concealed prejudices and emotions.

Interviewers should have more than casual knowledge of the important role in human motivation of influences other than the conscious and the rational. They should apply this knowledge not only to an understanding of their clients' personalities, needs, prejudices, and emotions, but also to an understanding of their own. The wise maxim of the ancient Greeks, "Know thyself," applies especially to interviewers.

The fact that an interviewer's attention must continuously be directed in two ways, toward himself as well as toward his client, sometimes makes him fear that he may become so overly self-conscious in his responses and may lose so much of his natural human warmth that his client will be alienated. But he soon learns to see the contrary danger—that spontaneous and unselfconscious response may be recognized by the client as only a surface response supported by such insufficient understanding of his real feelings that effective help will be impossible.

Another chapter is devoted to a discussion of the purposes of interviews, which take place for all sorts of reasons. At one end of the scale is the interview of the census taker, whose immediate purpose is simply to obtain specific information. At the opposite end is the definitely therapeutic interviewing of the psychiatrist or psychoanalyst. Between lie the vast majority of interviews, the aim of which is to help in one way or another, and information is sought primarily to direct this help to actual needs and to make it effective.

It is impossible to discuss interviewing in a vacuum. The specific techniques of interviewing vary of course with the purpose in mind. Because nearly all interviews involve the obtaining of information for the purpose of helping people, we use as typical examples interviews of this kind on a professional level, interviews characteristic of general social casework. Such interviewing furnishes rich material for a discussion of the nature and methods of the art. Another advantage of choosing this general field is that applications to specific fields of interviewing can readily be made.

Since we approach interviewing from its use in general casework practice, it is inevitable that some discussion of basic casework concepts will be included. But insofar as possible, our attention will be focused upon interviewing per se. We shall avoid discussing casework concepts as such because casework deserves a much more comprehensive treatment than would be possible here.

The general discussion of the methods and techniques of interviewing, though illustrated at each point, is supplemented by a section giving a number of interviews in more detail. They should also provide useful source material on which the experienced interviewer will wish to test his own procedures.

It should be clear that the discussion presented here gives but a selection of some of the most salient features of interviewing. They have been culled from a vast store of relevant knowledge accumulated over the years by professional workers in the casework field. Again, it should be noted that there is nothing sacrosanct in the order in which the various topics are treated. They are so interrelated that a discussion of any one of them involves some aspects of many of the others. In practice, things have to be said in a linear order rather than all at once, but it might be well to remember that an understanding of some of the topics treated later will help toward understanding the subjects discussed first.

2

Understanding Human Nature

There are certain basic facts about the nature of human beings with which every interviewer should be familiar. The different motives of interviewers will lead to different uses of such knowledge. The salesman, dominated by the profit motive, will use his knowledge of human psychology to increase his sales; the propagandist, whether his motives are good or bad, will use his knowledge to increase the infectiousness of his ideas. It is assumed that the users of this book will be motivated by the desire to be of service to their fellow human beings and will use their knowledge of human nature to that end.

HUMAN
MOTIVATION

The reasons underlying some forms of human behavior are obvious both to the actor and to outside observers. Sometimes they are concealed from outsiders but are recognized more or less clearly by the actor. Sometimes they are unknown even to him. For example, a man applying for a job insults his prospective employer. How can such behavior be understood? Did he not know he was being insulting? Or did he not know that an insult would prevent his being hired? Or did he not really want the job? Or what? In seeking to explain his failure to get the job, he might say, "The foreman was unreasonable." But very likely he would himself be aware of the unsatisfactoriness of such an explanation. Often people who behave in some such irrational way are as much puzzled by their behavior as is anyone else.

We can sympathize more readily with such a person's bewilderment if we realize that there is much of our own behavior we find hard to explain. Our glib rationalizations do not satisfy even ourselves. Why do we sometimes fly into a rage if we are kept waiting for a minute, when at other times we are willing to wait in line fairly patiently for half an hour? Why do we sometimes punish a child severely for a slight fault and at other times let flagrant misbehavior go unremarked? Why do some people in particular "get our goats"?

If we knew all, we would doubtless understand all. Bizarre behavior, like more usual behavior, has its causes, but sometimes they are deeply hidden. In dealing with others it is seldom possible or essential to understand fully the causes of their actions. It is essential, however, to realize that their behavior is motivated. Its source may lie in the depths of their personalities where neither they nor we can readily discover it. In a complex personality, with its many interconnected causal chains, the factors underlying a given bit of behavior are usually many and varied. A single cause cannot be isolated, and to attempt to force the individual to name one is to demand the impossible. He will be forced to resort to an inadequate rationalization.

The recognition that much human motivation is unconscious will enable the interviewer to be more tolerant, less condemnatory, and thus better able to help his client effectively. Instead of becoming impatient with rationalizations, he will realize that motives that the client disguises even to himself are probably sources of deep and painful anxiety to him.

Unconscious motivation is much more common than we ordinarily recognize in our attempt to understand people. We look too often for intellectual *grounds* for behavior rather than for psychological *causes* rooted in feelings and emotions. Drives are emotional in nature, and actions controlled by them have their source in feeling rather than in intellect. A person who apparently likes, but really dislikes, another "forgets" a luncheon engagement with him and in extenuation pleads a busy day. A man fired from a job because of incompetence "explains" that the work was too heavy for him. Why a client says certain things and leaves others unsaid, why a child with a high I.Q. fails in school, why a wife who effusively protests her love for her husband continually belittles him, are questions whose answers are to be sought not in intellectual but in emotional terms. Explanations such as "He's deceitful," "He's lazy," and "She's just being modest about him" are obviously inadequate. Yet for many people such remarks conclude the discussion and block any real understanding.

OBJECTIVE
AND SUBJECTIVE
ASPECTS

Every situation has its objective and subjective aspects. A man loses his job. That is an objective fact. His feelings about this event constitute a subjective reaction. A man is ill with tuberculosis. That is a medical fact. But every person who has any sort of illness has accompanying it certain feelings about the illness. There are variations in the physical aspects of tuberculosis, but there are many more variations in human reactions to that disease. Thus, we could run the gamut of human experiences and note that every objective experience—marriage, hunger, getting a job, leaving one's children in a day care center—has its accompanying subjective counterpart of emotional attitudes. Experience and skill lead to more and more awareness of this interrelationship.

Social workers sometimes contrast what they call the reality situation of a client with his emotional problems. This separation is unfortunate because it sometimes leads us to operate as if these two areas were mutually exclusive. The implication is that the emotional components of the situation are not real, whereas, of course, they certainly are real to the person experiencing them. The way one feels about a situation is as much a fact as the situation itself. To avoid such an erroneous implication, we shall, in this discussion, speak instead of the objective aspects and the subjective aspects of a client's situation. Both are always present.

If we seem in our discussion to be directing our attention primarily to subjective aspects, to feelings, attitudes, and emotions, it is because we recognize that they are as important as the objective facts themselves and are much more likely to be overlooked. Our concentration upon them does not imply any lack of appreciation of the significance of the objective facts. We recognize, of course, that too much attention to subjective factors would limit our service to the individual just as much as would lack of appreciation of them. In practice we must be extremely vigilant so that we give each group of factors its due weight.

A student who applies for a scholarship on the grounds that his father has just retired and is unable to see his son through college may be even more worried over his father's poor health, which necessitated the retirement, than he is over the financial problem. The dean who notes only the latter may be failing to give the boy the help he most urgently needs or may be giving a scholarship to a boy whose anxieties will prevent his profiting from it.

In seeking to help people even in very simple situations, we need to listen not only to their objective requests but also to the undertones that reveal their feelings and give us clues to perhaps even more serious objective situations not overtly revealed. A man's frequent absences from work may indicate neither unreliability nor laziness, but may be due to worry about his wife's illness or to anxiety about pressing debts. In either case the underlying subjective factor, worry, is caused by an objective situation that may not be apparent at once to a personnel manager.

Knowledge of subjective factors may be necessary to make possible the formulation of objective plans with some probability that they will be carried out. A Travelers Aid worker returning runaway Mary to her family in the Middle West knows that unless she talks to Mary long enough to find out her subjective attitude toward returning home, Mary may get off the bus at the next stop and foil the worker's plan for her safe return.

MORAL
PIGEONHOLING

In addition to recognizing the difference between objective and subjective aspects of a situation, the interviewer should recognize the futility and even the danger involved in passing judgment on people's attitudes. Although a mile may seem short to you, to tell a woman who has laboriously walked that distance that she should not feel tired is useless, to say the least. To tell an emotionally upset person that he should be calm may succeed only in erecting a barrier against further expression of his difficulties.

The thermometer of a room may read seventy-two degrees, but the room may feel hot to some and cold to others. A statement about the temperature can be objectively verified or disproved, but to argue about the heat of the room is futile. Disagreement in such a case reflects only differences in subjective feelings, and insofar as one reports them sincerely, one is reporting correctly.

Although we can judge statements about objectively verifiable matters to be true or false, we are not similarly justified in passing judgments on subjective attitudes. Of two people waiting in line, one may sincerely feel the delay to be an imposition, and the other with equal sincerity may regard it as a matter of course. The requirements for eligibility for financial assistance in a given agency may be objectively fixed, but to one client they may seem to involve an unwarranted intrusion into his personal affairs, whereas to another they may seem to represent only a wise, businesslike investigation. One applicant for a job may feel that the interviewer is prying into his private affairs; another, confronted by the same inquiries, may wonder why more information is not desired. Not the passing of judgment as to the rightness or wrongness of such diverse attitudes, but the understanding of their causes, should be the aim of the interviewer, for only the latter will be helpful to him in dealing with the situation.

In another area, too, there is a natural but unjustified tendency to judge actions right or wrong. For example, divorce is absolutely taboo in some groups, whereas in others it is expected to occur with a certain normal frequency. A "Down-East Yankee" would rather starve than borrow, but the average American, converted to installment buying, will purchase an auto with no down payment save his old car. But each group tends to regard its own views as correct, the one condemning divorce or borrowing as wrong, the other holding that, in certain cases at least, it is completely justifiable. Even legal attitudes change. At one period the sale of contraceptive devices is a crime and at another a legal enterprise. Social customs and laws change, and people alter their judgments of approval or condemnation.

It is essential for an interviewer to refrain from trying to impose his own moral judgments upon his clients. They should be allowed to discuss their feelings about pertinent matters without fear of condemnation. Knowledge of the flux of social attitudes on even basic ethical matters will tend to make an interviewer less absolute in his judgments of behavior. It would be desirable if he could refrain from making any such judgments about his clients, but since an interviewer, too, is human, he may find this godlike stance unattainable and discover that he does have strong feelings of condemnation toward some of their attitudes or behavior. The good interviewer will learn quickly, however, that any expression of such feelings blocks the progress of the interview. If his interest is genuinely centered in the client, he will learn to keep his own feelings in the background.

Wisdom will warn the interviewer also against hasty generalizations. He may tend not to trust in any matter a client who lies about his income and may regard as unreliable in other respects as well a youth who lies about his age in order to get a job. This all-or-none attitude permeates everyday thinking. People are regarded as all good or all bad, situations as completely right or thoroughly wrong. Such rigid classifications must be avoided by the interviewer who wishes to understand his client. He must recognize that there are shades and variations of rightness and wrongness. A person who lies about one subject may not lie about another. He may be so in need of a job that he will prevaricate no end to get one, but he may be scrupulously honest about financial matters. People who have fallen into "bad" modes of behavior in one field may be unusually "upright" in others.

"There is so much good in the worst of us, and so much bad in the best of us, that it ill behooves any one of us to find any fault with the rest of us." The truth of this saying is so obvious that we can be sure that any judgment utterly condemning another person will be mistaken. The all-or-none principle fails. But, on the other hand, it is probably a mistake to try to assess accurately just the respects in which a client is good and just the ones in which he is bad. It is much more important to understand him and to seek the causes of his behavior, even when it is antisocial, than it is to grow indignant about it.

CONFLICTING
PULLS

From birth on we have to make one choice after another. Some choices are relatively easy. In other cases we want very much to have our cake and eat it too. When forced to decide, we do so with much hesitation and often look back on our selection with some misgiving, wondering whether we have really chosen wisely. The student who gives up his fraternity beer party to study for an important examination feels the pull of the party very strongly while he tries to study. Sometimes the pull is so strong he reverses his choice and goes to the party, only then to feel the "voice of conscience" striving in vain to pull him back to his work.

In many cases we resolutely put the thought of what we have rejected out of our mind—that is, our conscious mind. But the pull of what we have denied ourselves nevertheless remains and sometimes takes its revenge in devious ways. When a choice has been hard, we cannot deny the attractiveness of what we rejected merely by saying we do not want it. We do want it. What is true is only that under the circumstances we want it less than that which we have chosen. We want to lie abed in the morning, but we want to keep our jobs more. We want to keep slender, but we also want to nibble sweets; and no matter which desire finally has its way with us, the defeated one is likely to rebel now and again.

Although some of us make up our minds more easily than others, we all experience many conflicting interests, desires, and emotions. The harboring of such conflicting feelings is technically known as ambivalence. An understanding of this concept is essential to anyone who is attempting to work successfully with people.

Sometimes an early conflict that was hard to resolve leaves us ambivalent about our choice long after the influences that led us to want what we rejected have ceased to exist. In such cases our ambivalence is not only unconscious but irrational as well. Nevertheless, it exists and has its adequate causes and its effects. Anyone who would understand our behavior today will do so more adequately if he at least knows in general of the existence of unconscious and irrational ambivalence, even though he may not know the details of our own case.

One common manifestation of ambivalence occurs in the areas of dependence and independence. Children want to grow up and have the privileges of adults—to spend their money as they like, to stay up late, and so on. At the same time they want to remain children—to play all day and to be free from responsibilities. This wish often carries into adulthood, so that even with chronological maturity many infantile desires continue to operate. Childhood food fads persist unchecked by adult knowledge. A man may marry primarily (though perhaps unconsciously) for mothering. It is only when the satisfactions of fulfilling adult responsibilities and obtaining adult privileges outweigh the desire for childhood pleasures that the individual grows up emotionally. All of us need to be loved, but for some of us this need causes conflict. We fear that accepting love will entail losing some of our cherished independence.

Superficial signs of dependence and independence are sometimes misleading. Here again we need to distinguish between objective and subjective aspects. A man may be self-sufficient, an executive, and still subjectively be weighed down by a longing for dependence, thus using up a great deal of emotional energy day after day in his efforts to maintain himself in his own eyes as an independent adult.

Instances of ambivalence arise continually in interviewing. They are manifested by clients who obviously want help but are unable to ask for it, who ask advice but do not utilize it, who agree to certain plans but do not carry them out, who say one thing but by their behavior indicate the opposite.

THE RELATIONSHIP BETWEEN INTERVIEWER AND INTERVIEWEE

Parents are often amused at the enthusiasm their young son shows for his schoolteacher. He reports her comments on the weather, imitates her mannerisms, wants to take her gifts, is delighted if she asks him to clean the blackboard for her after school, and so on. Another parent whose child has the same teacher may not understand why he seems negativistic toward all the teacher's suggestions and seems to go out of his way to annoy and irritate the teacher. Similarly adults themselves, when they stop to think about it, find that their strong attachments to or antagonisms for certain people seem unjustified by any conscious knowledge they have of the other's nature. Such positive and negative feelings toward those we come in contact with are, of course, universal phenomena, always present to some degree. Certain features of interviewing tend to intensify them, and for this reason the wise interviewer will want to understand their nature and effects and will seek to subject them to some measure of conscious control.

Understanding Human Nature
19

For many a client, talking with someone who listens with nonjudgmental understanding instead of criticizing or admonishing is a unique experience. This relationship with a person who does not ask anything for himself personally, but focuses his interest entirely on the client and yet refrains from imposing advice or control, is a very satisfying one. The discovery of these characteristics in the interviewer, accompanied as it is by the absence of closer knowledge of the interviewer's personality with its inevitable personal whims and foibles, leads the client to idealize him. The client's feelings are unchecked by personal knowledge of the interviewer that might dilute them. He thus endows the worker with the ideal characteristics one is always searching for, quite independently of whether the worker actually is such an ideal person.

These feelings are usually not consciously revealed, but indications of them may be recognized in such comments from clients as: "It's been such a help to talk with you," "I see you understand," "You're the first person I've ever told this to," "What do you think I should do?" Remarks of this sort occur frequently in interviews.

The opposite sort of situation also arises in interviewing. Again quite independently of the interviewer's actual character, the client, because of his own anxieties, insecurity, and deprivations, may endow him with negative characteristics and build up antagonism toward him. Much depends on the client's previous experiences with his parents or with others in authority. Negative feelings are often even more concealed than positive ones because of social standards of politeness, but they are revealed sometimes by the refusal to talk, by the breaking of an appointment, by refusal to return to the agency, or by trapping the worker into giving advice that can later be proved wrong.

The development of excessive negative or positive feelings by the client is often alarming to the interviewer who is unaware of having done anything to arouse such feelings. An interviewer tends to want his clients to like him, but sometimes in his eagerness to achieve this end he unwittingly encourages more dependency than he had realized was potentially present. A worker should realize that the development of an emotional rapport, positive or negative, between the client and himself is not abnormal but inevitable and that he should direct his attention not to eliminating this relationship but to controlling its nature and intensity. He must guard against misleading the client into an overly dependent relationship through appearing too personally friendly or appearing to promise too much, but he must not lean over backward in avoiding this danger and make the client feel that he is an unresponsive and unsympathetic listener. It is easy, when one is treated like a god, to assume a superior stance.

If an interviewer notices that the relationship with his client seems to be developing negatively, he should not become overly alarmed, because the client's attitude may be due not at all to the interviewer but to factors deeply hidden in his client's personality. He should review his own activity in interviews and make sure that he has given no objective grounds for the antagonism the client seems to feel toward him. He may have given inadequate help, broken an appointment, or himself have developed negative feelings toward the client of which he was not fully aware. If there are no such objective sources for his client's negativism, he can assure the client, by a continued attempt to understand the reasons for his difficulties, that he is not retaliating with disapproval of his own.

The development of an interrelationship of this general sort, positive or negative, between interviewer and interviewee is not at all a unique phenomenon but a universal one. It is essential that an interviewer recognize its existence in order to respond appropriately.

3

The Interviewer's Attitude

The importance of the interviewee's attitudes will have become clear by now. It is impossible to discuss the interviewee's attitudes and the conduct of an interview without commenting on the interviewer's attitudes at every point. All the things said about understanding human beings apply also to the interviewer, for he, too, is a human being, with unconscious as well as conscious motivation, ambivalence, prejudices, and objective and subjective reasons for his behavior. He brings to his relationship with the interviewee his own predetermined attitudes, which may profoundly affect that relationship. He has a natural tendency to impute to others his own feelings and may thus seriously misunderstand his client's situation and problem. If he is unable to bear frustration or poverty, he may find it difficult to comprehend his client's toleration of it. An interviewer who finds it difficult to reveal himself to others may decide that a client should not be "probed," when as a matter of fact the client wants nothing so much as to be helped to talk. We now discuss two of the many specific respects in which the interviewer needs to be particularly aware of his own feelings in order to be able to help the client satisfactorily.

PREJUDICES

Most of us often remark the prejudices of others but seldom are conscious of our own, for in our own case we regard them as natural opinions. When we are irritated or enthusiastic, when we react with anger, disgust, shame, pride, or love, it seems as if such situations would naturally cause such feelings in any normal person. A helpful step in discovering our own prejudices is to jot down a list of those we know others to possess. A little self-scrutiny will then convince us that these are not as alien to our own attitudes as we may have assumed.

We usually think of prejudices as large, overall attitudes, such as race prejudice, class prejudice, religious prejudice, and political prejudice. Here we are concerned rather with much smaller matters, subtler and more easily escaping notice. We find exaggerated dislikes of sloppy dressers, flashy dressers, skinny people, fat people, show-offs, weak men, aggressive women, blondes, brunettes, or redheads. Elsewhere we find exaggerated fondness for blondes, brunettes, or redheads, pipe smokers, women with slender ankles, or men with curly hair. Some interviewers prefer rather self-sufficient clients who state their cases incisively; others prefer meek clients who need considerable help to express their needs; few can avoid responding with warm satisfaction to "grateful" clients.

A comparison of our own list of prejudices with those of others will reveal the great variety in different individuals' attitudes toward the same sort of occurrence. For example, everyone has distinct ideas of his own as to what is really intolerable. Some can easily tolerate and attempt to understand the alcoholic but find a lazy person intolerable. For another laziness stirs no personal emotion but lying is an unpardonable sin: "I don't care what a person does so long as he is honest. I cannot bear to be deceived." Again, for others, even the most involved deception is passed over as a "white lie," but poor housekeeping is beyond the pale. A few find murder more easily acceptable than procrastination. Insofar as an interviewer can discover his own areas of intolerance, his own list of unpardonable sins, he has made a start toward self-disciplined control of his feelings in his relationships with others.

When an interviewer first learns that he should be nonjudgmental, should not become angry, should not become dependent upon the interviewee's affection and response, he tries to suppress his feelings, and as a result he tends to become artificial and stilted in his responses. It would be better to recognize the existence of such feelings and to learn to control their expression, for these feelings are not unnatural but merely inappropriate in the professional situation. If an interviewer is aware that he is becoming angry, he is then in a position to regulate his own feelings better than if he denies to himself that he has such feelings. Control of feelings rather than absence of feelings on the part of the worker is the goal.

ACCEPTANCE

We have spoken of the value of tolerance in an interviewer. But it is not easy to say how an interviewer can accept aberrant behavior or attitudes on the part of a client and yet maintain his own and the community's standards. Interviewers sometimes learn that they should be accepting without knowing very clearly what is involved in acceptance. Knowing the word gives them a false assurance that they understand its significance.

In the training of the individual, certain standards of behavior are inevitably imposed, first by parents and later by society. It is natural that the individual, in learning to condemn his own unacceptable behavior, should include in his condemnation similar behavior on the part of others. If, for example, he has learned to be neat, he tends to abhor slovenliness in others. The interviewer must learn to counteract this perfectly natural tendency to condemn all behavior that conflicts with his own standards. Toward almost every problem that a client brings, the interviewer has developed an attitude of approval or disapproval based on his own experiences, and he tends to assume that this attitude represents the norm. As his professional training and experience grow, he recognizes that there is a wide range of individual variation in human responses to a given situation. This recognition may lead him to try to accept all such behavior, to refrain from evaluating it carefully. But this reaction clearly reveals an extremely limited understanding of the concept of acceptance, involving as it does only an arid, nonjudgmental impartiality. Real acceptance is primarily acceptance of the feelings given expression by behavior and does not necessarily involve acceptance of unsocial behavior at all; real acceptance involves positive and active understanding of these feelings and not merely passive refusal to pass judgment.

A merely passive attitude of not passing judgment on a client's unusual behavior is often interpreted by him as a condoning of that behavior, a repudiation of a standard he himself accepts but has failed to live up to. He tends then either to reject the interviewer as an unfit guide or, at the other extreme, to continue and increase his undesirable behavior, thus trying out the interviewer to see how far he can go in his nonconformity. A man who makes no effort to get a job, for instance, may find his dilatoriness so accepted by the interviewer that he gradually gives up the struggle for self-maintenance entirely. A child whose petty stealing is ignored is not at all reassured, as he would be if he were confronted by the interviewer with knowledge of this misbehavior and yet convinced that in spite of what he has done the worker accepted him in the fuller sense of understanding his feelings and the emotional conflicts that induced his stealing. A child feels that a person who thus understands him is his friend. Such a person's recognition of his behavior will be regarded as a sign that he wants to help him overcome it.

To accept, then, is not to condone antisocial behavior but to understand it in the sense of understanding the feelings it expresses. In a worker's early acquaintance with a client it is, of course, impossible to know, let alone understand specifically, all the various factors responsible for given behavior. In such early stages we make use of the best knowledge we have available at that time, namely, the general familiarity we have acquired through theory and experience with the basic underlying dynamics of human behavior. We know that a person who appears angry and belligerent may, in fact, be feeling anxious and fearful, that one who appears demanding may have no other way to express his hurt pride and guilt about asking for advice or aid. Understanding of this sort lays the groundwork for real acceptance. As an interviewer's knowledge of the client deepens, however, his general knowledge is enlarged by an understanding of the particular pressures active in this specific situation. His general acceptance develops into more specific understanding. Such detailed understanding is not always possible, but the more definite it is, the more effective the worker can be.

Sometimes an interviewer, relying on his general understanding, says too readily, "I understand," and thus confuses and blocks the client in his attempt to present the details that would be needed for more specific understanding. The interviewer means that he wants to understand, or does understand in general, whereas the client realizes that he certainly does not yet know about the specific factors of his case. It often would be far better for the interviewer to say, "I do not understand"; then the client would realize that the interviewer wants to understand but needs more information.

Another easy error is to offer false reassurances. "I'm sure you'll soon be well." "I know you'll get a job soon." "Everything will be all right." Such remarks, far from reassuring the client, usually cause him to doubt the worker's understanding of the situation and consequently his ability to help. It would be more judicious and also more helpful to be realistic about the situation, to offer hope only when there are good grounds for it. The interviewer's recognition of the client's own doubts can itself be reassuring, for the client feels that he has in the interviewer someone who knows the worst and yet will still help him.

In the relationship between interviewer and interviewee,

intellectual understanding is clearly insufficient unless it is accompanied by emotional understanding as well. Intellectual knowledge may suffice for mathematics or logic, but to understand intellectually the successive movements of dancing or skiing does not qualify one as a good dancer or skier. Similarly, in our relationships with other human beings, intellectual understanding is barren unless accompanied by emotional understanding. To know about emotions and feelings is not enough. One should be able to sense their existence and their degree and quality. Such ability does not come merely from reading a book such as this one or from classroom study, but requires the constant application of theoretical knowledge in practical day-to-day contact with human beings and their objective or subjective problems.

The Interviewer's Attitude
29

4
Purposes of Interviewing

The method of conducting an interview will be influenced to a considerable extent by the purpose of the interview. As we have already noted, some interviews are directed primarily toward obtaining information, some primarily toward giving help; most, however, involve a combination of the two. The aim is to obtain knowledge of the problem to be solved and sufficient understanding of the person troubled and of the situation so that the problem can be solved effectively. Whether these two functions of understanding and helping are combined in one agency or interviewer or divided among several will modify the details of the methods used but not their essentials.

One early caution is worth noting. The interviewer is sometimes so anxious to help that he rushes ahead without first obtaining a sound understanding of the situation. That such a procedure can be destructive rather than helpful should be clear. To advise a young man to continue in college without first obtaining knowledge of his interest and abilities is obviously unwise. The first and basic purpose of interviewing is to obtain understanding of the problem, of the situation, and of the client who has come for help.

Another caution to be kept in mind throughout is that although the interviewer should be clearly aware of his purposes, it is not always wise to seek to realize them by direct action. Even when considerable information is desired, it is often best obtained by encouraging the client to talk freely of his problem rather than by asking such a pointed question as "Were you fired from your last job?" People are sensitive about their personal lives, family skeletons, poverty, past mistakes, and so on, and early flat-footed inquiry may only alienate a client and cause him to erect protective barriers against what may well seem to him unwarranted intrusion. Once convinced of the worker's sensitive understanding, of his desire to know not out of wanton curiosity but only in order to help, and of the confidential nature of the relationship, the client will welcome an opportunity to talk about things that earlier he would have suppressed.

The specific kinds of help an interviewer can give, and consequently the specific sort of information he will seek, are determined to a considerable extent by the functions of his agency. He may, for example, want to obtain the kind of information that will be needed to give medical aid, or the kind needed for financial assistance, child placement, or employment. Within this general field he will be guided by the indications his client gives him of the special facts involved in this particular case. He will first listen to his client's statement of his needs and then guide the interview along those channels that seem most appropriate to the specific circumstances of the situation. A good general alters his strategy for reaching a given objective according to changes in the situation, and a good interviewer will modify his techniques as circumstances demand.

The information to be sought by an interviewer is sometimes fixed in advance by a printed form or specific instructions from the interviewer's superior. In such cases it is essential that the interviewer be thoroughly acquainted with the purposes back of each question and understand its significance. Otherwise he tends to ask the questions in a perfunctory manner that minimizes their importance to the interviewee and raises doubts as to the significance of the interview. Further, an interviewer is inclined to accept superficial and inadequate answers to questions whose purport he has not grasped. Unless he understands the purpose of obtaining certain information or carrying out certain plans for the client, he will frequently be unable to do either effectively.

For example, an interviewer asked simply to obtain a developmental history of a highly distressed man who has suddenly left his job may do so in a perfunctory manner that will miss many significant details. If, however, he knows some of the ways in which a psychiatrist may use such information in helping a man who has had a sudden breakdown, he will be able to do a much more adequate job.

The interviewee, too, should be helped to feel that each question is important and significant. In addition to the presence of this conviction on the part of the interviewer, it may be necessary to explain, in a way that will satisfy the interviewee, the relevance of the questions to his own needs and interests. A question as to one's birthplace may seem irrelevant until one realizes its importance in determining citizenship. A question as to what floor the client lives on assumes more significance if he is afflicted with a heart ailment; questions about diet are called for when a person has tuberculosis; early developmental history has special significance in children's behavior problems; the number of jobs held in the past ten years is important in gauging a man's employability.

Every interview has, to begin with, its manifest purpose. If an agency has initiated an interview and called someone in, the person interviewed can usually be put most quickly at his ease—relieved of uncertainty in the face of the unknown—and the interview most quickly advanced by a straightforward statement, in terms the client can readily grasp, of the interviewer's purpose in asking him to come in for a consultation. When the interviewee asks for the appointment, the situation is a little different. In such cases, rather than greet the client with a barrage of questions, it is better to let him state in his own words his problem and his purpose in coming in for an interview. Sometimes the client is nervous and incoherent, but he is most quickly reassured if he is allowed to begin the interview in his own way. Often the interviewer can learn much from the very hesitancy and indirect way in which the client approaches the account of his difficulty.

The worker will, of course, keep in mind the specific functions of his agency, because these may delimit rather sharply the area in which he can be of service. Sometimes he can help most by referring the client to some other agency whose ability to aid will be more pertinent to his needs. Ordinarily, however, even a referral should not be made immediately, for often the manifest purpose of the client differs considerably from his real purpose, and the latter may well fall within the field of the given agency or require referral to a quite different agency from the one that first comes to the interviewer's mind. A woman with three children applying for a job may need first of all an opportunity to clarify her own thoughts as to whether she wants to work and place her children or whether she wants to seek financial assistance from a public welfare agency in order to maintain her home. Only after this question has been settled can we know where to refer her.

Most people who come seeking help or advice are considerably troubled by their problems, as is evidenced by the fact that their anxieties have risen to such a pitch as to drive them to take the step of seeking this consultation. This anxiety may make it difficult for them to see their problems distinctly or state them clearly. Very often their problems will be so involved that they are unable to come anywhere near locating the root of the trouble. A man who comes in to register for a job may really need medical attention. A woman who expresses anxiety about the development of her children may have more real need to discuss her troubled relationship with her husband. And so on.

The inexperienced interviewer should keep in mind the possibility that his client is suffering from some trouble more difficult than he realizes or is able to state. He will endeavor by various methods to put his client at ease, to stimulate him to talk relatively freely about his problem, and to help him to organize his own confused thoughts and feelings about his difficulties. Sometimes talking about the situation to a sympathetic listener will itself lead to a satisfactory conclusion. The client's thoughts may thus be organized so clearly that he himself sees what action he should take. His fears and hesitancies may be removed, and he may be encouraged to take whatever action is necessary.

More often, perhaps, just talking is not enough, and help of other sorts will be required. We shall discuss some of these subjects later. Our purpose now is to call attention to the desirability of looking beyond manifest purposes to more fundamental latent ones that may be present.

It is, of course, possible to probe too far. Some sleeping dogs should be left undisturbed, particularly when the interviewer is not equipped to deal with them should they be aroused. Even a skilled interviewer should use a good deal of discretion and wisdom in going beneath the surface.

The fact that interviews bring to light new knowledge of purposes and needs as well as new information about the relevant facts implies that the interviewer should not let his plan of action be unalterably fixed in advance or determined early in the interview. A certain amount of flexibility is always desirable.

5

🌿How to Interview

Although the most skillful interviewing gives the appearance of being a smooth and spontaneous interchange between the interviewer and the interviewee, the skill thus revealed is obtained only through careful study and years of practice. For purposes of study it is possible to break down an interview into a number of component parts and discuss each separately. In actual interviewing, of course, no such sharp breaks occur, but we must make them in analysis if our discussion is not to be so general as to be relatively useless. The interviewer must become conscious of the various subtleties in interviewing before he can absorb them into his spontaneous responses. First recognized in theory, they later become so much a part of the worker's skill that they are utilized naturally at each step without conscious notice.

36

We hear much of the intuitive skill of the trained interviewer. But back of such skill lies much study of the various
processes and interrelationships involved in interviewing.
The skillful skier is unconscious of the many movements
integrated in his smooth flight, but earlier he had to learn
them painfully, one by one, and then learn to combine them
into a harmonious, coordinated whole.

One danger that arises from an analytical treatment
such as we must necessarily undertake is that an interviewer,
in his attempt to find a few simple rules that will guide him,
will seize upon certain techniques that are highly valuable
in certain cases and apply them in others in which they are
less relevant. Supervisors notice that words of a caseworker
reported in a case and discussed favorably in a staff meeting
begin to recur time and again in the reports of their young
students. We should remember that each technique suggested has its limitations and should be used only on appropriate occasions and in conjunction with other techniques
that are equally demanded by the whole situation. In practice none of the methods to be discussed operates in a
vacuum, but only in organic relation with most of the
others.

OBSERVATION

In one sense all that we shall say about interviewing
might well come under the heading of observation. Here
we shall discuss a few of the simpler and more obvious
types of observation important in all interviewing. It goes
almost without saying that we should observe what the interviewee says. It is less obvious that we should note equally
what he does not say, what significant gaps there are in his

story. We should note also such things as bodily tensions, flushing, excitability, and dejection because they supplement, and sometimes even belie, the picture given by the client's words. The following opening sentences of the report of an interview reveal how much is told by the physical behavior of the client:

Mrs. Marsh came to the office asking for temporary financial assistance. I noticed her sitting in the waiting room before my interview with her. She was sitting erectly, almost rigidly, and was clenching her hands in her lap. Her face was white and drawn. When she came into the interviewing room, she was so tense and nervous that she could hardly speak. She sat on the edge of her chair, looking directly at me and wringing her hands. A large, well-built woman with blonde hair, extremely blue eyes, and light skin, she appeared to have a severe case of acne, which marred her complexion. When I asked Mrs. Marsh to tell me how I might help her, she spoke in short, jerky sentences and told her story in no logical sequence.

Out of all the things to be observed, each interviewer will remark only a relatively small number. His selection will be determined by his own observational equipment as limited by his interests, prejudices, attitudes, and training. Since it seems impossible to make note of things without adding a personal element of interpretation, he may even modify considerably in his own picture of the situation the data actually presented to him. To illustrate this influence of the observer's own nature on his reports, the following experiment is sometimes conducted in an early session of a casework class.

Students are asked to write, in not more than a page,

an observation they have made of an individual or a group of individuals. The observation may take place in a restaurant, at a bus station, on the street, or on the campus. Students are asked to perform this experiment in pairs; two students observe the same scene and write it up without comparing notes. These parallel papers are then read in class. Such a project is unusually convincing in illustrating the subjective variations of the observer. Sometimes the reports are so different that the students cannot believe they are of the same situation. In one an individual is described as angry, callous to the pleas of his child for an ice-cream cone. In the other he is reported as anxious, uncertain, indecisive, frustrated, and helpless in the face of a demanding offspring in a temper tantrum. A project of this sort directs a student's attention to the limitations of his own capacity to see what is actually happening and to his tendency to distort the objective facts with his own preconceived ideas of what he himself would feel or do in such a situation.

That we cannot take for granted that our observation of an individual is accurate is initially a blow to our self-confidence. It is a blow, however, that may help to break down any preconceived ideas about our infallibility and pave the way to self-scrutiny and the development of a more observant capacity to size up situations as they really are. It comes at first as a surprise that what seems like anger to one person may be sensed as anxiety by another. What seems like cocky self-assurance to one may be sensed as tense insecurity by another. What seems like "sweetness and light" to one may be recognized as hostility by another. Such differences in interpretation arise partly from the facts that people do not always behave and act as they feel, that they do not always say what they really mean, and that they do not always behave logically and rationally. But in part they are due to the fact that everyone necessarily looks at the rest of the world from his own immediate point of view, which always seems to him the natural, logical, sensible one. When an interviewer realizes that a client's point of reference seems like the reasonable one to him, it becomes clear that it is important to attempt to understand how the situation looks from his viewpoint and why that seems to him to be the only correct way of looking at things. If we attempt to see the client's point of view before trying to persuade him to accept what seems to us a more logical point of view, we may have a faint beginning of understanding him.

Many times a client finds in the interviewer the first person in his experience who can listen understandingly and yet not intrude upon his feelings or attempt to redirect his behavior. This experience for the client is sometimes surprisingly satisfying. As just noted, it alone is sometimes helpful. At other times it is merely one part of a helping process.

That people do not always say what they mean or act as they feel is continually apparent in interviewing. For example, caseworkers in public welfare agencies repeatedly have the experience of having a client storm into the office belligerently demanding immediate financial support, only to have him reveal, when met with kindness, that underneath he is really frightened, ashamed of his poverty, and pleading for understanding of the trouble in which he finds himself.

LISTENING

One type of observation occurs through listening, which is one of the fundamental operations of interviewing. It goes without saying that a good interviewer is a good listener, but what constitutes a good listener? One who frequently interrupts to say what he would have done under similar circumstances is not a good listener, but neither is he who sits like a bump on a log. Absence of response may easily seem to the talker to reflect absence of interest. Everyone knows from his own experience in telling a story that people like a listener who indicates by brief relevant comments or questions that he has grasped the essential points of one's tale and who adds illuminating comments on certain significant features of one's account that have not been stressed and might well have been overlooked by an inattentive listener. This attention to important details that have not been emphasized gives the storyteller the stimulating feeling that the listener not only wants to, but does, understand to an unusual degree what he is trying to say.

A common error of an inexperienced interviewer is to be embarrassed by silences and to feel that he must fill them with questions or comments. A decent respect for silences is often more helpful. Sometimes the person interviewed falls silent because he is a little reluctant to go on with what comes next in his story or because he does not quite know how to formulate what he plans to say. A too hasty interruption may leave this important part of the story forever unsaid. Sometimes, of course, a silence is due to other causes and, if allowed to continue, will only embarrass the person interviewed. In such cases a pertinent remark or question will encourage him to continue.

Listening to a client's story is sometimes helpful in and of itself. Everyone knows the value at times of "letting off steam." When something happens that upsets a person or "makes him mad," he tends to get over these feelings more quickly if he can find a sympathetic friend who will let him "rave" for a while. Relieved, he can then go ahead and use his energy more constructively. Without this opportunity to talk it out with someone else, he may "boil" for days. He probably does not want anyone to tell him what to do or what he should have done differently but may merely want someone to listen and understand how upset he is. It is unfortunate that the average lay person is not a good listener. He usually feels impelled to point out the other person's mistakes and faults or to give advice about what to do.

The following report of an interview from an employment agency illustrates how valuable mere listening can be:

Mrs. Cobb came in to register for a job, but there was such difficulty with simple matters, such as name, address, and former jobs, and she seemed so upset that I said perhaps she felt these details were not important, and possibly we should talk about a definite job for her first. She said she did not mind very much about answering the questions, but she did not know what she would do if she should get a job. I asked how she meant this, and she said that everything at home was all upset and it kept her worried all the time. I replied that many people felt they could talk only about employment when they came to this agency, but we were interested in helping people in every way possible, and I knew there were many things besides a job that could be worrisome. She said that I had "certainly told the truth that time" and proceeded to tell a very long and involved story about many troubles with her husband, children, death in the family, and so on. When she had finished, I said that she certainly had had many troubles and I should like to help her if she felt there was something I could do. She said she thought she could manage everything by herself, but that day she had been walking all over town worrying to herself and was "nearly crazy" and felt she just had to talk to somebody. She said that she did not often get this way, but when she did she just had to talk to someone. After she talked she always felt better, but she felt best when she talked to somebody who knew "what it is all about." I said that we had used up a great deal of time and that there was someone else waiting to see me, but I should be glad to make an appointment for her to come back to talk either about the job or something else we might be able to do for her. In preparing to leave, she said she did not think it necessary to come back because she thought that things were going to be better and she had a part-time job that helped out with family expenses. She seemed much more cheerful than when she came in, and I remarked that I was glad we were able to help her even if all we gave her was conversation. She replied that I was still young and some day I would learn that "conversation is a wonderful thing."

There is, however, a danger in allowing the client undirected expression of his feelings. They may be due not to a recent upsetting experience but to a long chain of experiences going back into the remote past. These early experiences may have become twisted and distorted and interrelated with other things through the years, so that mere talking does not bring relief. His need to talk may not be occasional but constant, and if the interviewer encourages too much release of feeling, areas may be opened up with which both interviewer and client are unequipped to cope. In general, catharis through talking is more effective the more the disturbing feeling is related to a fairly recent experience, and it becomes of dubious value the more the feeling is due to long-repressed experiences. If a difficult situation can be immediately aired, the danger of its being pushed from consciousness but remaining an active source of anxiety is lessened. If a person has had a hairbreadth automobile escape, he feels better if he can talk about it a lot for a while, for then its importance gradually wanes and is forgotten. Particularly with children, it is helpful to remember that if they do have a traumatic experience—an accident, an operation, a sexual assault—the more immediately they can be helped to express their feelings about it, the less will be the danger of its becoming a source of neurotic conflict. It is as if the wound should be kept open long enough to drain off the infection in order to avoid a festering sore.

A USO worker reported the following incident:

A young soldier, asking for information about a place to eat, seemed nervous and upset. He lingered after the worker had given him the information, and she asked him if there was anything further with which she could help him. He said there was nothing else but went on to say that he supposed he had to eat but didn't feel like it. He had been upset since morning, when he had lost his buddy in a fatal accident during maneuvers. He described in detail how his friend had been run over by a tractor, and went over again and again the gruesome details of the accident he had witnessed. The boys had come from the same state, where they had gone to school together. They had entered the army at the same time and had always been inseparable. He seemed to get some relief through talking about it and said, when he left, that he felt "a lot better."

LISTENING
BEFORE TALKING OR
"BEGIN WHERE THE
CLIENT IS"

The first step in an interview is to help the interviewee relax and feel fairly comfortable. Naturally it is difficult to help the interviewee relax unless the interviewer himself is relaxed. Sometimes the client can quickly be put at ease by letting him state his purpose in coming, sometimes by giving him a brief account of why he was asked to come. In either case an advisable next step is to encourage him to talk and then to listen carefully while he speaks of what is on the "top" of his mind in connection with the interview. Listening to the client gives the interviewer a chance to become acquainted with him, to know what language he speaks, literally and figuratively. It makes clear the kind of questions, comments, and suggestions that should later be directed to him and the way in which they should be formulated. It is as unsatisfactory to use literary language with a person used to the vernacular as it is to use slang expressions with a professor totally unfamiliar with them.

Even when our primary interest in a given interview is to obtain the answers to a set of questions, we can profit much from letting the client talk rather freely at first. He will usually reveal the answers to many questions without their being asked and often will suggest the best methods of approach for obtaining any additional information that is required.

When suggestions are to be made by the interviewer,

it is even more important to let the client express himself first. Sometimes he will even suggest the course of action that the interviewer intends to advise. In such a case his own suggestion can simply be confirmed and strengthened, and the fact that he regards it as coming from himself will make it more likely that he will carry it out. In other cases the client may reveal a deep-seated hostility to the suggestions about to be made, and in such cases the interviewer is warned to proceed with caution and to attempt to discover and remove or modify the emotional causes back of the hostility before proposing his plan.

Another advantage in letting the interviewee talk first is that it tends to counteract any preconceived ideas about him that the interviewer may have allowed himself to entertain. It gives the interviewer the immense advantage of being able to see the situation and the client's problem from the client's point of view. Because it is the client who eventually must act, it is obviously advantageous to start from where he is rather than from some vantage point of the interviewer, even though the latter might be superior.

If someone comes in and asks for a job and the interviewer proceeds at once to make a number of suggestions, he may well be surprised later to find that the client has adopted no one of them. Upon further examination the worker may then find out what he might well have discovered in the first interview if he had done more listening and less talking—that the client's real worry was that he could not hold a job if he got one, or that he did not see how he could take a job because his wife and children were sick at home and needed constant care.

QUESTIONING

Perhaps the central method of interviewing is the fine art of questioning. We shall discuss only a few of its many features.

Abrupt or tricky questions are inappropriate in a casework interview. The method of the casework interview is the method of friendliness, the method of asking questions in order to understand and be of assistance. Clients soon recognize the attitudes of their interviewers and tend to respond to the best of their abilities when they feel the presence of a real desire to understand and to help.

The interviewer who puts his questions accusingly or suspiciously arouses only fear and suspicion, not cooperation. The wording of the question is often of less importance than the manner and tone of voice in which it is put. The interviewer's safeguard here is really to be interested in understanding and aiding; then his manner and tone are very likely to reflect that interest. The question, "Are you looking for work?" may sound suspicious, accusing, sarcastic, or friendly, depending upon how it is expressed, and that expression in turn reflects how the interviewer really feels.

Questioners who are beginning to find out about the influence of unconscious desires and emotions on human behavior sometimes come to enjoy so much the discovery of some hidden motive or influence that they cannot resist letting the client know that they "see through" him. They experience the joy of the amateur detective and, by revealing this attitude, alienate their clients. A more mature understanding would lead them instead to feel increased sympathy with a person in such distress that he had been forced to conceal important facts even from himself.

A similar error consists in becoming so interested in the mysterious realms of the unconscious that the interviewer probes his client unnecessarily to satisfy his interest in the esoteric. Though probing for a bullet is pretty painful, mental probing can be far worse, and realization of this fact should cause an interviewer to carry his inquiry only as far as is necessary for him to be effectively helpful.

A good general rule is to question for only two purposes—to obtain specifically needed information and to direct the client's conversation from fruitless to fruitful channels. Examples of the latter would be questions that encourage him to talk in relevant areas in which he finds the going difficult and remarks such as "I don't quite understand," which will help him to elaborate more fully.

Most people tend to ask either too many questions or too few. Each interviewer should study his own tendency and seek to curb it. Too many questions will confuse and block the client, whereas too few may place too much of the burden of the interview on him and may leave salient areas unexplored.

In general, leading, rather than pointed, questions and questions that cannot be answered by a brief "yes" or "no" are to be preferred. They stimulate the client to talk freely and avoid the always present danger of putting answers into his mouth. Even if questions that imply an answer do not result in false answers, they tend to give the impression that the questioner is lacking in fundamental understanding of the situation. "Would five dollars be enough?" is not as good a query as "How much do you need?"

A questioner should, of course, try to adjust his pace to that of his client. To go too slowly suggests lack of interest or understanding. To push ahead too fast is to miss important clues, to confuse the client, and to suggest in a different way that we are not really interested in what he has to say. Again, we must accept the client's pace in the sense of not pushing him to reveal more than he is prepared to at any one time. To ask him to reveal confidences before we have won his confidence is to court defeat.

There are no magical questions that can be used on all occasions as the good fairy uses her wand. Sometimes in reading a case record, a student comes across a question that was so timely and effective that he is tempted to use it in his own next interviews and is surprised that it does not bring the same rewarding results. In general, we seem to get further by being encouraging and sympathetic, by leading the client to talk freely, than by trying to drag information out of him by belaboring him with questions.

TALKING

Closely allied to questions are the comments of the interviewer. Sometimes the only difference between the two lies in the speaker's inflection. "You found your last job pretty difficult" is either a query or a comment, depending on whether one raises or lowers the pitch of the last syllables. In any case both questions and comments are species of talking, and certain rules hold for both. In general, the interviewer should comment only for purposes similar to those for which he asks questions—to reassure or encourage the interviewee, to lead him on to discuss further relevant matters, and so on. The one additional kind of talking that goes beyond these purposes is the definite giving of information or advice. As suggested earlier, this stage should come after the interviewer is familiar enough with the client's situation to know whether suggestions will be acceptable or pertinent.

Many years ago the Travelers Aid–International Social Service of America (then called the National Travelers Aid Association) issued the following suggestions to its workers under the title of "The Art of Giving Information." These comments are as valid today as when they were written in 1941.

There is a real art in giving information. The volunteers must be interested in giving it. A perfunctory response will keep the inquirer from asking other questions or even from repeating his original question in case he has not understood the answer. A bored expression is obvious to other people nearby and may cause them to decide from the volunteer's manner whether they will avail themselves of her service. A cordial manner, such as one would use in meeting guests, is desirable. In fact, people coming to a TAS desk are in a sense guests of the TAS for the moment. A pleasant, gracious greeting and a pleasant "May I help you?" will encourage questions, while a taciturn, gloomy expression and no word of greeting will repel them.

Written directions, if they are at all complicated, are preferable to those given only verbally but often there is not time to write them. It is always wise to have the person repeat the directions if there is not time to write them out.

The volunteer will soon learn that the first question is often only a "trial balloon" asked while the questioner gathers courage to ask the thing he really wants to know. This is another reason for the friendly, inviting impression which the volunteer must make. If the question is asked in a hesitating, halting manner, or if the person lingers, or if he turns away in an undecided manner, the volunteer has a responsibility to help the questioner by some such remark as "Is there something else you wish to ask about?" or "Maybe my answer wasn't clear to you." It must be remembered that many of the people who ask questions are not sure of themselves and so may not be direct about their questions. The volunteer must be sure, therefore, that she understands the question as well as that the questioner understands the answer.

There is a great difference between expressing a meaning and communicating a meaning. Since the latter is the aim of the interviewer, he must devote considerable care to his manner of expression. He must "think with wisdom" but speak the language of his client, including as far as possible the idiom of the client.

So often words used by one group are not understood by another. This tendency not to be understood is obviously true of technical words, such as resources, siblings, and eligibility, and of the specialized terms of such fields as law, medicine, and psychiatry. But also many everyday terms are used with quite different senses by different people. A person given to exaggeration may describe as "catastrophic" an event that another would call "a slight accident." The difficulty of transmitting meaning is aptly illustrated by questionnaires. How many who have filled out the pesky things have ever understood all the questions? An interviewer who remembers his perplexities on such occasions can readily sympathize with his clients and even anticipate some of their difficulties.

It is not enough that all the words used by the interviewer should be understood; it is important also that they be understood as they were meant. For example, many caseworkers bandy about such terms as love, hate, anger, and hostility in a loose way, meaning to include weak emotions as well as strong ones, whereas to many a client anger involves at least such overt phenomena as flushing of the face, clenching of the fists, and rapid increase of heartbeat and respiration. The worker who tells his client, "I know you were angry with me for missing our last appointment," seems to the client to be grossly overstating the case.

ANSWERING
PERSONAL QUESTIONS

Interviewers are frequently troubled by the personal questions clients ask them. Sometimes they are embarrassed and do not know what to answer or indeed whether to answer. If we can judge correctly the reasons back of such questions, the appropriate response will often be indicated.

A client may ask personal questions merely because he wants to be polite or thinks it is the social thing to do. He may not be interested in the answers, and in such cases if the discussion is directed back to his own problems, he will be glad to continue with what is to him a much more absorbing subject, himself.

Often such questions as "Do you play bridge?" "How old are you?" "Are you married?" may indicate simply the interviewee's natural curiosity about the person to whom he is in turn telling so much.

Again, personal questions may indicate the beginning of the establishment of that closer relationship between the interviewer and the interviewee discussed in chapter two. The interviewee is interested in finding out something about the personality and interests of the interviewer. He is testing him out, wanting to know what sort of person he is in order to know whether his real personality corresponds to the one the interviewee is beginning to picture in his mind.

In most instances a brief, truthful answer to a personal question is desirable. Normally the answer should be followed by an immediate redirection of the client's attention to himself. One danger is that the interviewer, through embarrassment, may become involved and tell too much, more than the client is really interested in knowing. This kind of response directs the client away from his own problems rather than toward them.

At other times an interviewer becomes involved in personal questions because he has failed to grasp their significance. Often such queries are not really personal but constitute rather the client's way of introducing a problem of his own that he would like to have discussed.

An older adolescent boy absorbed with the problem of whether to marry may be trying to give the worker an indication of this concern and his desire to discuss it by a question, "Why aren't you married?" A brief impersonal answer leading to a question about his own ideas about marriage will open the way for the client to pursue his own problems, which may involve such things as worry over leaving his mother or fear he cannot support a wife.

Attractive young women interviewers occasionally find it difficult to maintain a professional relationship with a male, especially an adolescent boy or an older man. In their eagerness to be helpful they sometimes overrespond and, without realizing it, lead the interviewee to believe that they are personally interested in him. Then they are very much embarrassed when asked for a date. They have failed to make clear in their manner the professional nature of the relationship. Had they done so, the interviewee, though attracted, would have gauged the interviewer's interest correctly as a friendly desire to help.

When such misinterpretation of the professional nature of the relationship does occur, instead of becoming frightened and withdrawn, the interviewer can best handle the situation by frankly telling the client that she feels she can be of most help if she sees him only during interviews and if they direct their discussion primarily to his difficulties. At the same time she should scrutinize her own attitude to make certain that she has not fallen into certain mannerisms that would lead a client to expect too much from her.

Sometimes an interviewer deliberately introduces his own personal interests into the discussion. He may admire the interviewee's flowers or dog and add comments about his own likes and dislikes. Or to encourage the client to talk about his early experience, he may tell the client that he, too, is from Texas and reminisce with him about the locality and people mutually known, or he may even enter into a discussion of politics, unions, or religion. Although at times such devices may be successful in helping the interviewee to feel acquainted and relaxed, the value of their use, except in rare instances, is dubious. Their dangers outweigh their possible value. With the introduction of the interviewer's personal opinions and feelings, the relationship may leave the professional level and become a social give-and-take or, worse, an argument. It is better for the interview to proceed with the client as the focus of attention, for his ideas and opinions, rather than the interviewer's, are paramount in the professional relationship.

Interviewers sometimes make the error of trying to win the client's approval by commenting on the attractiveness of his clothes or the appearance of his home. There is a distinction between an honest, natural appreciation of such things and flattery or patronage. If the interviewer's interest is genuine, an expression of it may help in furthering the interview, but if it is a technique whose purpose is to flatter the client, this artificial intrusion will be sensed by the client. A saccharine effusiveness on the part of the inter-viewer is as offensive to a troubled person as irritability.

LEADERSHIP
OR DIRECTION

From all that has been said thus far it may seem as if the interviewer assumes very little activity and direction, since so much stress has been put upon leaving the client free to express himself in his own way. Indeed, the inexperi-enced interviewer often feels as if the client were running away with the situation—setting the topics for discussion and determining the pace of the conversation—so that all the poor interviewer can do is to keep track of what is being said. Actually, however, the skilled interviewer does assume leadership throughout. He consciously decides to allow the client to express himself. He knows the function and policy of his agency; he knows, in general, the areas in which he may be of service to the client; and with these things in mind, he guides the conversation along paths that enable him to determine whether he is going to be able to help the client and, if so, in what respects. He first directs his ques-tions along the lines of allowing the interviewee to express his need in sufficient detail so that he may understand him better and know whether he will be able to help or whether he will need later to refer the client to someone else. He unobtrusively directs the interview throughout, deciding when to listen, when to talk, what to observe, and so on. With the overtalkative person who is inclined to ramble, or the person whose mind tends to wander, he gently and sympathetically leads the interviewee back and redirects him through leading questions to a discussion of the im-mediate situation.

The difficulty in acquiring the appropriate degree of leadership in interviewing is well illustrated by the following report from a beginning student of casework:

At first I seemed to be off somewhere when opportunities presented themselves to guide the client in expressing his feeling at a given moment. I sat like a stick, and when later asked by my supervisor why I had not done this or said that, I answered, "I don't know." Then I went to the opposite extreme. I progressed not only to the point where I learned to insert "Why?" but I carried questioning so far that often, as was pointed out to me later, I had switched what was on the client's mind to some other track. However, I am learning to listen again. It's a different sort of listening than I did when I sat petrified lest by speaking I stop the client's flow of conversation entirely. It is a more intelligent listening that is the outgrowth of the little bit more assurance I have. I am beginning to listen because I realize it is what my client wants, rather than because I do not know what to say that may help him express himself. If I do ask a question or say something, it is to show him I understand or want to help him say what he is finding it difficult to tell me and not, as previously, because I am shaky in my position and feel I have to say something so he'll know I am there and that I am the interviewer. You learn and learn, and what remains to be learned seems to grow and grow.

The question of what material is relevant is not so simple as it might seem. Frequently material that seems irrelevant to the inexperienced has, because of the common tendency to disguise and distort and misplace one's feelings, considerable significance. It may be necessary to let the client ramble on for a while in order to clear the decks, as it were, so that he can get down to things that really are on his mind. On the other hand, with an already disturbed person it may be important for the interviewer to know when to discourage further elaboration of upsetting material, especially if the worker would be unable to do anything about it. An inexperienced interviewer might, for instance, be intrigued with the bizarre elaboration of material that the psychotic produces, but further elaboration of this material might encourage the client in his instability. A too random discussion may indicate that the interviewee is not certain of the areas in which the interviewer is prepared to help him, and he may be seeking some direction. Or again, satisfying though it may be for the interviewer to have the interviewee tell him intimate details, such revelations sometimes need to be checked or encouraged only in small doses. An interviewee who has "talked too much" often reveals subsequent anxiety. Such a reaction is illustrated by the fact that after a "confessional" interview the interviewee frequently surprises the interviewer by being withdrawn, inarticulate, or hostile or by breaking the next appointment.

In certain types of interviewing the interviewer is called upon to give advice and to offer suggestions, sometimes to formulate concrete plans of action and even to bring some influence to bear on the client to adopt a plan of procedure. It is always a problem how far direction of this sort should be carried.

The interviewer in a social agency is there primarily to serve the client. His problem is how best to make his help effective. Many of his clients come seeking advice. They feel that a person in the interviewer's position is equipped to give expert advice, and they expect that when they ask for it, it will be proffered them. If the interviewer has sound advice to give and if his client is free enough of conflict to be able to accept it, it is probably wise to offer it. In many cases, however, advice is futile because the client is unable to act upon it. A woman in emotional conflict over her husband finds it difficult to accept advice either to divorce him or to remain with him. We can point out in such cases the probable consequences of the various alternatives that are available and stimulate the client to a course of reflection that may enable her to reach a decision for herself. For example, we can make clear the possibilities of getting a job, the legal procedures that would be necessary for a divorce, the steps to be taken in getting public assistance, the possibilities of aiding her husband to make a better home adjustment, and so on.

Frequently people who ask for advice really do not need it. Usually they have had plenty of that from relatives, neighbors, clergymen, or doctors. What they need is assistance in freeing themselves from some of the confusions in which they have become bogged down—additional information that will throw light on their situation and encouragement to come to a decision of their own.

There are times when it is helpful to give a bit of advice to the client who demands it in order to test out his ability to use it, to challenge the mobilization of his energies so that both he and the interviewer may see more clearly whether he is able to profit from suggestions. Again, a bit of harmless advice may merely be a symbol to the client of our interest in him and willingness to try to help, whereas our rigid refusal to make suggestions may seem to the client an unwillingness to help.

Frequently the client who asks, "What do you think I should do?"—even the client who comes in with an eviction notice and seems to dump it helplessly in the interviewer's lap—when questioned as to whether he has any plans actually has several resourceful ideas. If a worker who is asked for advice gives it because, perhaps, he fears that if he did not his prestige with the client would be threatened, he is really failing to utilize the client's own resourcefulness. In a surprising number of instances, the client who in turn is asked, "What do you think?" comes forward with ideas and plans of his own.

It is still more difficult to know when, if ever, an interviewer should go so far as to try to persuade a client to a course of action that he is reluctant to adopt but that seems to the worker clearly indicated. "A man convinced against his will is of the same opinion still." Many a persuasive interviewer has been disappointed by subsequent events. A foreign-born mother who is afraid of hospitals but who is persuaded to take her sick child to one blames the interviewer if the child dies after she has removed him from the hospital at a critical period against the doctor's advice. Yet it would be as much a mistake not to offer such a mother the opportunity of medical care for the child. There is a distinction between persuading people against their will and generously offering them concrete help. One ought not simply neglect problems of health, budding delinquency, or the poverty of those too proud to ask for help. Of course, in certain agencies that have a primary responsibility to protect the community, the situation is quite different, and even forceful measures may be in order.

The casework interviewer should remember that his primary aim is to help his clients. If this desire is his basic driving one, he need not be overly fearful that he will appear too inquistive or too authoritative. There are occasions, especially in certain types of cases, when an interviewer represents some degree of authority to the client. If, however, his feelings are centered on the welfare of his client, this fact will break through the barrier of his authoritative position and be recognized by the client. If, on the other hand, the interviewer is absorbed in his own fears that the client will not like him and hence will not talk, or will regard him as prying, then indeed the client will sense the interviewer's uncertainty and come to distrust his motives.

When possible, it is, of course, desirable not to appear to exercise authority, but to lead the client to take for himself whatever steps are necessary. In general, the things people do for themselves have more meaning for them.

If people find their own jobs, look for their own housing, make their own applications to hospitals or other agencies, they are more likely to carry plans through. One person's way may not always be the same as another's, but each person has to work out his own manner of meeting situations. We must allow people a large measure of self-determination.

On the other hand, a worker should not allow his theory of self-determination to become a cloak behind which he withholds giving the client the help really needed. It is possible to give so little direction that the client profits not at all and is not even helped to know what kind of assistance is available.

INTERPRETATION

The interviewer's first aim, as we have said repeatedly, is to understand as fully as possible his client's problem. To achieve this understanding, he must interpret the many clues to the underlying situation that the client presents through his behavior and conversation. Rarely is the client sufficiently conscious of his own self to know and be able to give a straightforward account of the crucial factors that lie at the base of his difficulty. The interviewer must discover these factors himself by going beneath the surface of his client's remarks and understanding their more than superficial significance. Just as a physician must look beyond the symptoms, say, fever or a bad cough, to the cause of his patient's illness, say, pnuemonia or tuberculosis, so the casework interviewer must look for the underlying anxiety or fear that is symptomatically indicated by hostility or dependency or chronic invalidism.

Juvenile stealing, for example, may express merely a desire to be "one of the gang," or an unrealized need for revenge because of harsh home discipline, or, of course, any one of many other things. Failure in reading on the part of a boy with a high I.Q. may be due to poor eyesight but is more likely to be a consequence of some emotional conflict, such as ambivalence about growing up or fear of competition with a younger sister.

The experienced interviewer will constantly be framing hypotheses as to the basic factors in the case confronting him, testing these, rejecting most of them, tentatively retaining others, seeking further confirmation, and so on. For example, when a woman in speaking of her husband "accidentally" refers to him as her father, the alert interviewer notes this reference but does not jump to the conclusion that her relationship to her husband is to an unusual degree that of daughter to father. He recognizes this idea as one possibility and keeps his attention open for corroborating evidence. In practice many of the tentative hypotheses one forms have to be discarded. Flexibility, the ability to change our hypothesis with the appearance of new evidence, is a trait well worth cultivating.

For an interviewer to interpret for himself is essential; for him to pass his interpretations on to the client is usually inadvisable. It is tempting to reveal our discoveries, for example, to say to a client, "Your blustering shows that you are really afraid." But if an interviewer is interested in helping the client, he will ordinarily keep such interpretations to himself. A client can profit from the interviewer's insight only if it becomes also the client's insight, and this transfer cannot usually be made in so many words. The client must arrive at his own conclusions at his own pace. To be told that he feels anxiety, rejection, fear, and so on, will not help him. He must come to recognize the existence of such feelings himself with sufficient conviction so that he can voluntarily acknowledge their presence.

Once an interviewer realizes the existence of such underlying factors, he can often help his client to a recognition of them through discreet questions and comments, which include some element of interpretation. A client who is afraid to talk may be encouraged by a query such as "You are not quite sure I understand?" or by an interpretative question such as "You are afraid I will blame you as your mother has always done?" This last question would be appropriate only if the client had already been able to express fairly freely his feeling of rejection.

In general, by encouraging a client to elaborate more fully, the interviewer helps him see for himself the relationships between the various things he has said. A man may talk freely about his hatred for his father and again about his "so and so" boss. A worker will have helped him understand, that is, to interpret the situation, if he can be led by further discussion to a recognition of the connection between these two hatreds. Often interpretation consists in opening lines of communication between two previously isolated compartments of thought.

In a few cases in which a secure relationship has been established between client and interviewer, we may wisely proffer a more direct interpretation. If a puny, precocious "mother's boy" looking longingly at a group of boys playing baseball remarks, "I don't like baseball," we may perhaps say gently, "You really mean that you would like to be out playing with them, but that they don't like you?" We would do this, however, only if we were sure that the boy felt certain the worker liked him. In such a case the worker's expression of this thought for him might well be a relief. It would indicate to him that the worker really understands him and that it is not necessary for him to make painful admissions. If the worker had made such a comment early in his relationship with the boy, it would have appeared only as an accusation to be resisted. A sense of proper timing is important for an interviewer. Often what cannot be said earlier should be said later. With regard to many questions or remarks, it is not a matter of their goodness or badness but of their appropriateness at a given time.

Very often it is unnecessary ever to bring to a client's clear consciousness truths about himself of which the interviewer has become fully aware. It is important to remember that an interviewer's goal is seldom, if ever, to achieve a complete personality change in the client. As a result of changes in little ways and of slight modifications of attitude, people often come to be able to make their own decisions and work out their most pressing problems without having become consciously aware of the many factors that the interviewer may see in the situation.

6

What to Look for in Interviewing

It will be helpful for the reader to devise some method of studying interview records, his own or others. One helpful device is to use various symbols (checks, asterisks, x's) to identify the more important aspects of interviewing to which attention has been called. The interviews of part two furnish good material for such an exercise.

For instance, with one symbol identify every recorded instance of the worker's activity, including gestures, questions, and comments. These passages may then be studied more readily to note the amount and kind of worker activity. Were the comments made to obtain further information, to encourage elaboration, to reassure, to indicate appreciation of the client's meaning, to restate and emphasize, or to refocus attention and redirect the course of the interview? Do they block or confuse the client or indicate understanding of him? Do they probe too deeply, proceed too fast, become argumentative or sarcastic, or are they sympathetic and appropriately timed?

We may also want to check and consider other aspects of interviewing. The following list is only suggestive. In addition to the items mentioned, we may want to examine an interview for certain specific points, such as mention of financial need, alcoholism, job experiences, and illness.

ASSOCIATION
OF IDEAS

The phenomenon of free association is well known to the lay public. It has been publicized by William James under the name of stream of consciousness and by such fiction writers as James Joyce and Ernest Hemingway. It is worthwhile to be aware of its operation both in the client and in the interviewer. When the client mentions something, such as lying, divorce, a grandmother, there may be started in the interviewer a stream of association that has little to do with the client's feelings about these topics. The interviewer must recognize his own associations because otherwise they may operate unconsciously. That is, he may read into the client's problem feelings that he has but that the client may not have. On the other hand, if he listens for the client's own free association, he will gain many helpful clues about the things he is discussing. A father may be telling about his son's running away and, instead of continuing logically in this discussion of his son, may begin telling

What to Look for in Interviewing
65

about his own youthful runaway escapades, indicating that to him his son's behavior is not a separate episode but is entangled with his own feelings carried over from his childhood. A mother may be telling about her inability to get along with her husband and switch suddenly to talking about her parents' separation when she was a child and her unhappiness and shame about this situation, thus indicating that her own current problems are not isolated but are connected in her mind with her parents' similar difficulties.

SHIFTS IN CONVERSATION

It is frequently difficult to understand why a client suddenly changes the topic of conversation. The reason often becomes apparent through study of what he was previously saying and the topic he begins to discuss. The shift may be an indication that he was telling too much and desires not to reveal himself further. It may be that he was beginning to talk about material that was too painful for him to pursue, perhaps too personal or too damning. On the other hand, it may be that what seems to the outsider as a shift in conversation is really a continuation, that in the unconscious of the client the two discussions have an intimate relationship. For instance, the interviewee may be discussing his difficulties with his foreman and suddenly begin discussing his childhood and the beatings his father gave him. The relationship in his own mind between his foreman and his father becomes obvious. Or he may be discussing his mother and suddenly make a personal remark about the woman interviewing him, indicating that in his own mind she in some way reminds him of his mother.

OPENING
AND CLOSING
SENTENCES

The first words a client says are often of unusual significance. Even though they are about the weather, they may indicate some reluctance to accept the professional nature of the interview and a desire to keep it on a polite, social level. Frequently the way in which a client first expresses his request gives the key to his problem and to his attitude about seeking help. He may start with "I don't suppose you can help me but . . ." or "I came because So-and-So sent me." The manner in which he states his problem always bears special study.

Concluding remarks are also noteworthy. Often a client's last remark indicates either his summing up of what the interview has meant to him or the degree to which his own forces have been mobilized for going ahead and working out his problem.

RECURRENT
REFERENCES

In studying interviews we often notice a recurrent theme. A client repeatedly returns to a certain subject. This reference may be specific—a job, his need for money, his difficulties with his wife—or it may be more general. For example, we may detect throughout an interview repeated indications of difficulty with authority. The client complains about unjust treatment from his landlord, his father, his wife, and so on. Another person may reveal the theme of inability to express hostility. We may note that he is continually denying his own irritation. He starts to complain and then makes allowances.

Similar to repetition is the situation in which the client "talks in circles." He talks freely enough but does not move forward. He repeats the same ideas over and over. A man complaining about unfair treatment by his employer repeats and repeats his complaints, unswerved by the worker's explanation of his possible misinterpretations. A mother tells over and over again the story of her childhood or of difficulties with her husband. Such circularity presents a stumbling block to an interviewer. When we have become aware that such an impasse has been reached, it is necessary to devise ways of inserting something new into the ritual, thus breaking up the circle and transforming it into a spiral. Here the interviewer's choice of a subject to insert is often guided by clues the client has given, perhaps some topic that has been mentioned before but not explained. If we have no clue, we may even have to make an insertion blindly, by trial and error. Questions such as "What would you like to do about it?" or "How would you like to have your husband act?" may stimulate the client to move into new and more profitable areas of discussion.

INCONSISTENCIES
AND GAPS

We may note that the client's story is not unified. He often contradicts himself. His real meaning is not clear. Such behavior may indicate the operation of such internal pressure as guilt, confusion, or ambivalence.

A man may report that he finished high school and

later tell how he has had to work full time since the age of ten. Another may seem sincere in his statement that he is bending all efforts to find a job and yet be unable to mention specific places where he has applied.

Or again, a client may tell a straightforward story but with unexpected gaps, areas in which the interviewer finds it impossible to elicit information. Frequently these areas are of particular importance. A man may carefully neglect to give any reasons for leaving his last job. A woman may discuss in great detail certain difficulties she has been having with the children but say nothing about her husband. The significance of such gaps or inconsistencies often becomes clearer through their cumulative force. One such occurrence may suggest a barely possible interpretation. But if ten others confirm this hypothesis, it is no longer a mere possibility but a probability.

CONCEALED MEANING

It is essential for the interviewer to accustom himself to listening to what his client means as well as to what he says. The little boy who does not like baseball is clearly suffering from "sour grapes," since he is friendless and unable to get along with children of his own age. Usually, however, the presence of concealed meaning is not as obvious as in this instance, and often it is only with the most careful observation of slips of the tongue and attitudes and other clues that the interviewer can obtain any increased idea of the client's total meaning. An unmarried mother who protests that she does not even want to see the father of her baby again may be concealing her infatuation for him and her hurt that he has "left her in the lurch."

Sometimes clients practically announce the presence of

concealed factors. A woman may say, "I don't know whether it's a job I'm worried about or other things." In a first interview it might be wise to concentrate attention on the job, but at a later stage it would be well to inquire about the "other things."

A fine example of concealed meaning is furnished by the following incident:

At an afternoon tea in New England, attended by members of both sexes, a woman made a remark to the effect that the English public school system tended to make men brutal. All in this group took sides, some agreeing and some disagreeing with the generalization. A heated and lengthy discussion followed in which the merits and demerits of the English public school system were thoroughly reviewed. In other words, the statement was taken at its face value and discussed at that level. No one, seemingly, paid attention to the fact that the woman who made the statement had married an Englishman who had received an English public school education and that she was in the process of obtaining a divorce from him. Had it occurred to the others, as it did to one person in the room, that the woman had expressed more clearly her sentiments toward her husband than she had expressed anything equally clear about the English public school system and that the form in which she expressed her sentiments had reacted on the national and international sentiments of her audience, which they, in turn, had more clearly expressed than anything equally clear about the English public school system, such an idea would have been secretly entertained and not publicly expressed, for that is the nature of polite social intercourse.

But in an interview things are otherwise. Had this statement been made in an interview, the interviewer would not have been misled by the manifest content of the statement. He would have been on the alert for a personal reference, and, once he had learned about the woman's husband, he would have guided the conversation on this topic rather than on the English public school system. Furthermore, he would have been on his guard not to allow any sentiments which he as a social being might entertain toward the English to intrude into the interview.[1]

[1] F. J. Roethlisberger and W. J. Dickson, *Management and the Worker* (Cambridge, Mass.: Harvard University Press, 1939), p. 273.

What to Look for in Interviewing

7

Essential Conditions of Good Interviewing

There are certain more concrete details in interviewing that should not be overlooked. Understanding and skill may be invalidated unless certain specific preparations are made for interviewing and certain precautions are taken. These may be listed under the general headings: (1) Physical Setting of the Interview, (2) Recording, (3) Confidential Nature of the Interview, and (4) Background Knowledge of the Interviewer.

PHYSICAL SETTING

The physical setting of the interview may determine its entire potentiality. Some degree of privacy and a comfortable, relaxed atmosphere are important. The interviewee is not encouraged to give much more than his name and address if the interviewer seems busy with other things, if people are rushing about, if there are distracting noises. He has a right to feel that, whether the interview lasts five minutes or an hour, he has the undivided attention of the interviewer during that time. Interruptions and telephone calls should be reduced to a minimum. If the interviewee has waited in a crowded room for what seems to him an interminably long period, he is naturally in no mood to sit down and discuss what is on his mind. Indeed, by that time the primary thing on his mind may be his irritation at being kept waiting, and he frequently feels it would be impolite to express his annoyance. If a wait or interruptions have been unavoidable, it is always helpful to give the client some recognition that these are disturbing and that we can naturally understand that they make it more difficult for him to proceed. At the same time, if he protests that they have not troubled him, we can best accept his statements at their face value; further insistence that they must have been disturbing may be interpreted by him as accusing, and he may conclude that we have been personally hurt by his irritation.

The length of the interview is, of course, so dependent upon the purpose of the interview that no optimum period of time can be fixed. In casework practice, however, it has been found that there is a great advantage in having the client know ahead of time that he will have a certain amount of time by appointment and that he may use it all or not as he wishes. In some agencies interviews are as brief as fifteen minutes; in others longer periods are necessary. In general, it is seldom helpful to have the interview last more than an hour. Interviews lasting several hours exhaust both client and worker. They may indicate that the client has been

Essential Conditions of Good Interviewing
73

trapped into telling more than he wanted to or that the interview has been inefficiently conducted so that too much time has been consumed in rambling. The fact that the client knows that his interview will terminate at a definite time may stimulate him to organize his material and present it concisely. Rather than have too long an interview, it is probably wise for the client to have time to digest and think over what he has said and what has been said to him. After the lapse of an interval permitting the client to reflect, a second interview will be more effective. It gives the client a greater sense of direction and security if he and the interviewer fix a definite time for the next appointment rather than leaving it to him to "come in again some day."

It is desirable for an interviewer to have time between interviews or during the day to think over each interview quietly and note any significant aspects of it. Though efficiency is important, it cannot be measured by the number of interviews conducted within a given period. Rather, efficiency in the interview relationship is proportional to the adequacy of understanding that is obtained, understanding that will make effective help possible. In the long run the greatest efficiency will be achieved by giving the client comfortable surroundings, undivided attention, and ample time to express himself during the interview.

The discussion thus far has assumed that most interviews will take place in an office. There are, of course, many instances in which interviews are of necessity or from choice conducted elsewhere, for example, in the home, at a person's place of employment, or in a school.

An office interview has obvious advantages because it provides opportunity for quiet and freedom from distracting interruptions. In addition, it is frequently preferred because people who seek out help for themselves are generally more likely to make use of it. The initiative required to leave the home and go to an office is often an indication of the client's ability to exercise some self-direction.

The fact that a client's willingness to leave home frequently indicates whether he is motivated does not mean, however, that we should make it a universal rule to refuse to visit clients. There are times when the client is unable to come to the office, and there are other times when he needs help and may later be able to bring himself to seek it actively. If the interviewer is rigid in his refusal to leave the office to offer his services, he may lose an opportunity to help when he is really needed. A person's failure to come into the office may have been due to his ignorance of the nature of casework service. In such a situation a "sample experience" of what the agency can offer, as demonstrated in a visit to the home, may alleviate his natural distrust of the unknown.

RECORDING

If an interviewer can set aside a few minutes immediately after each interview for jotting down full notes concerning it, he will be saved the necessity of making many notes during the course of the interview itself. It is always something of a question how much note taking during an interview is wise. There are usually certain factual things— names, addresses, dates, ages, places of previous residence or employment, and so on—that are normally written down as soon as they are mentioned. The interviewee regards it as perfectly natural for them to be noted and is not disturbed by the momentary pauses needed for writing them out.

If note taking goes much beyond this point, however,

the interviewee may easily feel that he does not have the interviewer's full attention and may be distracted from the normal progress of his account. Similarly the interviewer's own participation may be interrupted or blocked by the exigencies of writing. Certainly when dynamic material is being revealed, the full attention of both interviewer and interviewee should be on the material itself. Even when an interviewer has an outline that must be filled in, he does not need to do so slavishly in one, two, three order. Often the answers to many questions come out naturally in the course of the interview and can be inserted later.

A beginning interviewer may need to make a number of notes as he goes along. An open notebook in which these may be jotted down unobtrusively is of great help. With practice he finds that he can rely increasingly on mental notes rather than on written ones. Just a word or two in the already open notebook suffices to enable him to recall a whole phase of the conversation. With still more practice he finds that he can recall in amazing detail the full course of an interview.

The all too common carry-over from college of the practice of filling notebooks with devitalized details must be given up and replaced by understanding listening combined with guiding participation. An interviewer's primary attention should be not on the future record to be made of the interview, but on putting the client at his ease, encouraging him to talk freely, guiding his conversation into the desired paths, interpreting and reinterpreting the clues given by his words and behavior—in short, on understanding his situation and his need and on thinking about the most effective ways of helping him.

CONFIDENTIALITY

When a person goes to a doctor or a lawyer, the confidential nature of the relationship is well established. The confidential nature of the interview relationship is often less well recognized. When it is established, beneficial results accrue at once. Frequently, after some reassurance as to the confidential nature of the interviews, the interviewee is able to go ahead and talk freely about what is troubling him, even giving information that, if generally known, might involve him with the courts or create further family discord.

If interviewers are to build up respect for the confidential nature of their relationship with clients, they must in practice warrant this respect. As has been suggested, because of the relationship between the interviewer and the interviewee, the interviewee is often led to reveal himself more fully than he has to others, and it is the interviewer's responsibility not to misuse these confidences. It is sometimes tempting to use incidents from an interview as anecdotes in a social gathering of colleagues or lay people. This practice may seem harmless because it does not directly affect the client, but actually it should be avoided, for it gives the impression to others that we take the confidences given us lightly. Often, too, such careless talk suggests that our attitude toward our clients is a patronizing one.

Many agencies have strict rules against removing a record from the office, not only because of the danger of its loss but also because of its confidential nature. It goes without saying that a case record should be perused only in private. The subway or a bus is no place to read a case record, even though one is hard pressed to find time to read it in the office.

BACKGROUND KNOWLEDGE

There is a certain body of knowledge, some specific and some general, that is the responsibility of an interviewer to possess. The specific knowledge concerns the special purposes of the agency with which he is connected. An information clerk in a department store has to know where to direct anyone who wants an article sold in the store, but she would not be failing in her responsibility if she did not know the transportation schedule to a suburb. An interviewer in a public welfare agency has to know eligibility requirements but does not have to know, as an interviewer in an employment agency does, the skills required for various jobs. A Red Cross worker has to know many army regulations not needed by a worker in a child-placing agency. The amount of such specific information required is often considerable, but it varies greatly from one agency to another. On the other hand, there is a more general body of knowledge that every interviewer, no matter what agency he is associated with, should command. Such knowledge would include, at a minimum, the topics discussed in this book.

PART
TWO *Illustrative*
Interviews

The discussion of the following interviews is presented not as exhaustive but as suggestive. It will be helpful if the reader, before proceeding to the comments about each interview, will note in his own mind what he regards as the significant points of the interview in order to compare his views with the discussion that follows. If his own thinking does not follow the lines of this particular discussion, there is no reason for surprise or concern. There are many different ways in which these interviews might be considered, and each individual will inevitably make his own selection of certain points for special emphasis.

The primary objective is to learn to analyze interview material and to think constructively about it rather than merely to absorb "the story" in a passively receptive way. Any method that promotes this active thinking about the interviewee's problems and interviewing techniques is helpful. One method, that of checking the material for a number of crucial factors, has been mentioned in chapter six.

If this were a book about casework, the discussions of the interviews would have to be carried much farther. Those who are interested in casework will find it helpful to supplement their thinking about the interviewing methods by a consideration of the casework principles involved.

One of the illustrative interviews is from fiction, and ten are from the records of social agencies. In the latter, all names and identifying information have been disguised.

8

🌿 "Only a Conversation"

An interview from fiction provides a convincing illustration of some of the points discussed. Whereas in real interviews we have a report of only the client's observed behavior, in fiction the author is able to present the subjective feelings of the person. The additional subjective material the author gives us is frequently just what the interviewer is seeking to obtain from the client.

The following interview illustrates many of the salient features of interviewing that we have discussed:[1]

To-day, as always on the days when the cannery was closed, Mrs. Kazalski wavered between relief at having free time for housework and distress at the loss of a day's earnings. Good,

[1] Viola I. Paradise, "Only a Conversation." Reprinted by permission of author and publisher from *Atlantic Monthly*, January 1923, pp. 81–93.

at least, that the weather was fine, she thought; and told Katie to take her cough out into the sunshine, and to see that the baby did not cut himself on the oyster-shells. Then she sent Dan to the pump, at one end of the "camp," for water, and turned to sort an accumulation of soiled clothes, which smelt unpleasantly of stale oyster-juice.

Mrs. Kazalski accepted the distasteful odor with a dull fatalism, as she accepted the rest of her widow's lot: as she accepted everything in her life. A careless observer might have called her broad peasant-face stupid, might never have guessed that the thick crust of acceptance covered a shrinking sensitiveness, and had nothing to do with her thoughts. These, in so far as she thought at all, concerned themselves with obvious things: Worry over Katie's cough, the debt at the company store, a mingled hope and dread of the early call of the factory siren on the morrow; for an early siren meant a big load of oysters, and consequently more nickels.

She had put the clothes in to soak, when she became aware of excitement in the camp, and the sharp voice of Mrs. Oshinsky's Annie in breathless recital. Mrs. Kazalski put her head out of the door, and saw a group of women and children—Katie among them—at the end of the building.

One of the women called her, and in the next sentence told Mrs. Oshinsky's Annie not to talk so loud. She arrived in the midst of the hushed importance of Annie's outpouring.

"Gov'ment ladies. It's men dressed like ladies. Two. One went to talk to the boss. Mike Salinsky says it's inspectors. The other went down to the lower camp, but she says she ain't a inspector. She'll be here after a while. If they catch on us kids is working, you got to pay fines. Twenty-five dollars, Mike says. He says the gov'ment pays them to be inspectors, and that's why things cost so much at the store. He's awful mad. He says if it wasn't for inspectors, everything would be better for us. He says maybe they'll take the work away from us. He says maybe they'll put us in jail. I think maybe they got revolvers—"

.   .   .   .   .

After some discussion, Mrs. Kazalski spoke.

"It ain't nothing. They can't take money we ain't got. If we keep our mouths shut, they won't know the children work. The cannery ain't running to-day. Everybody's got to tell their children to shut up, and to shut up themselves, only be polite. No gov'ment lady or man neither won't get something out of me."

All morning, as she worked, however, she worried about the "gov'ment lady." Suppose that someone should let it out! Jail? No, surely not that. But if they should stop the children from working, how could they live? Suppose the company should refuse credit at the store! Once she had wished to cheat the Virgin Mary of a half-burned candle. Could this be punishment?

And suddenly, athwart her numb acceptance of life, came a passionate regret: if only she had never left Baltimore! Why, why, had she yielded to the persuasions of Mike Salinsky! She went over in her mind all the incidents that had influenced her to "come South to oysters." The day of Mike Salinsky's visit stood out as clearly in her mind as if it had been yesterday, instead of the day of her husband's funeral, three months ago.

[The story continues with Mrs. Kazalski's introspection as she goes over in her mind all that has happened between the time of the funeral, three months ago, and today. She thinks of how she sat after the funeral, dazed, wishing only to be alone, but being pestered by her sister-in-law with "What are you going to do now?" At last the sister-in-law

"*Only a Conversation*"

85

left and then suddenly there appeared the smooth, oily, but persuasive Mike Salinsky with the offer: "How would you like to go South? How'd you like to go to the Gulf of Mexico, down in Mississippi where it's nice and warm, and where you and all the children could get nice easy work, and good pay, and free rent, and free fuel? How'd you like to go South and shuck oysters and pick shrimps for the winter? I'm row-boss for the O. U. Oyster Company, and they sent me up here to get families to come down and work." It was particularly the lure of the warm South and his assurance that Katie's cough would get better there that finally persuaded her. She recalls all the awful disappointments upon her arrival. The miserable one-room accommodations in a long, sagging twelve-room row, the back-breaking work, the change in Mike to a brutal boss, prodding her and the tiniest child through the long working hours, the high prices at the company store and the ever-increasing debt piling up there, and above all the worry over Katie's increased coughing. Now, added to these conditions was the agonizing fear that the government ladies would find out about the children's working.]

Mrs. Kazalski struggled hard against despair. If only she had never left Baltimore!

And now the government, the government was sending inspectors, to fine them, to starve them, to take the work away from their children! Twenty-five dollars! Suppose they discovered that her children worked, that she had not the twenty-five dollars? Some of the neighbors might let it out. Well, the government lady would get nothing from her, not a thing. She would be civil, but not a word about the work!

The government lady was in the door. "It's not a man, dressed as a woman," was Mrs. Kazalski's first thought. "Annie Oshinsky is a fool!" She responded, unsmiling, to the

"Good afternoon, Mrs. Kazalski. I'm Miss Egmont of the Children's Bureau. May I come in?"

"Sit down," she said in a dull voice. But she thought, as she looked at the short, slight, brown-clad figure, the pointed piquant face under the close-fitting little round hat, "She looks—almost—as if she could be happy!" It came as a revelation to her that any adult could look like this.

Afterward, thinking of her, Mrs. Kazalski wondered why she had seemed so remarkable. She was not pretty, nor yet clever: apparently she had not noticed Mrs. Kazalski's hostility, had acted as if she were welcome. She had said, easily, "May I take off my hat? It fits a little too tight"; and, without waiting for permission, had removed it and hung it on the knob of the chair.

Afterward, as during the interview, Mrs. Kazalski felt about in her sparsely furnished mind for a word to explain this visitor, so unlike anyone she had ever met. The Polish word for "separate" kept coming to her mind; but, being unused to abstract thinking, she did not recognize it as exactly the word to express Miss Egmont's detachment—detachment for herself, apparent freedom from problems of her own—which was a quality that puzzled and attracted Mrs. Kazalski.

Mrs. Kazalski's reflections about the worker reveal that the interviewee as well as the interviewer is observing, sizing up, speculating. We note Mrs. Kazalski's recognition that the interviewer has not responded to her hostility or retaliated in kind. The interviewer's first activity indicates an easy relaxation. She asks, "May I come in?" "May I take off my hat?" but proceeds unhesitatingly to do both without waiting for an answer. Mrs. Kazalski's rather incoherent thought of the interviewer as somehow "separate" shows that she recognizes that her questioner is not using this occasion for personal gratification but is primarily interested in her. This mutual interplay constitutes the beginning of the establishment of the interviewer-interviewee relationship. Miss Egmont is sensed by Mrs. Kazalski as being a person free of all problems. Actually she undoubtedly has, as does everyone, worries of her own, but Mrs. Kazalski senses that she does not let them intrude into the interview.

This interview has a certain special interest in view of the fact that the government lady represents authority and must begin the interview by forcing herself upon another person. It illustrates how she overcomes this initial handicap, and later developments show that in spite of it she is able to be of real help to Mrs. Kazalski.

"Did you ever hear of the Children's Bureau?" began Miss Egmont. And when Mrs. Kazalski had said, "No'm," she continued, "Well, it's a part of the government that is trying to find out how children and mothers are getting along, and what they do, in order to learn what things are best for them. Now we are visiting all mothers with children in these little canning camps. How many children have you?"

Mrs. Kazalski was immediately on her guard. Miss Egmont's pencil was poised over a large card, on which Mrs. Kazalski could see irregular patches of printing, combined with blank spaces, and red-and-blue ruled lines. Miss Egmont was not looking at the card, but at her hostess, with half-smiling encouragement. And surely, thought Mrs. Kazalski, that was a harmless question. No harm, either, in giving their ages, and telling at what grades they had stopped in school. In fact, Miss Egmont turned directly to Katie and Dan, who stood by, their wide eyes upon her, and asked them questions about school. Katie, who coughed most of the time, *coughed harder now, from nervousness; and Miss Egmont's face clouded, as she asked about the cough.*

Because Miss Egmont has sought out Mrs. Kazalski, she begins the interview with a brief explanation of the purpose of her visit. Notice here that she does not confuse Mrs. Kazalski by a long and involved explanation that would at this point be meaningless. Later, as we shall see, when it has more meaning, Miss Egmont gives a fuller explanation. Here her simple, straightforward account not only serves to give Mrs. Kazalski an intellectual understanding of the reason for her visit but also, by its informality and friendly tone, serves to reassure Mrs. Kazalski and to indicate that the interview will be not a third degree but a mutual discussion of a common problem.

The interviewee's sensitiveness to minute details is illustrated by her noting that Miss Egmont, though asking questions from a card, was looking at her rather than the card. (A client once told her family caseworker that she would not go back to the public welfare agency because the worker there "did not even look at me but just wrote down the answers I made to her questions.") The sense of receiving the full attention of the interviewer encourages conversation and accelerates the progress of the interview.

Miss Egmont "begins where the client is"—that is, she begins with simple, innocuous questions that stimulate Mrs. Kazalski to talk and do not frighten or threaten her by seeming to plunge too quickly into "dangerous" areas. Mrs. Kazalski is naturally unready to talk freely until she has had an opportunity to acquire more confidence in the stranger. In every interview there are simple "identifying information" questions that can be used as a springboard from which to progress to more important matters. They serve as an opportunity for interviewer and interviewee to get acquainted and to test each other.

Despite her resolution to be circumspect in her dealings with this intruder, Mrs. Kazalski scarcely listened to what she was saying, so preoccupied was she in her personality. "If she had my life and my troubles," she thought, "would she be so—so different?"

"You 'Merican lady?" she asked.

"Yes," said Miss Egmont, "but my grandparents came from the old country. How long have you been in America?"

"Nine year. How old are you, lady?"

If Miss Egmont was surprised, she did not show it. "Thirty-two," she replied. "And you?"

Mrs. Kazalski's eyes opened wide. Thirty-two! Why, she herself was only thirty. She would have guessed Miss Egmont fully ten years younger. Then surely this apparent happiness was not real. Why, she was not married: was an old maid. Mrs. Kazalski softened, with something like pity. So busy was she speculating about her visitor, that she answered questions mechanically. But suddenly, one question brought her up short.

"Now tell me about the children's work. I suppose Katie can't help you very much at the factory, because of her cough?"

Mrs. Kazalski's face hardened. She made no answer. Miss Egmont might ask till doomsday, she'd get nothing out of her. Yet it was strange that she should ask the question so directly—not at all as if she were trying to surprise an answer from her.

Mrs. Kazalski inserts a personal question, "You 'Merican lady?" It is an expression of her natural curiosity and of the beginning of the relationship being established between them. Miss Egmont answers matter-of-factly and contributes additional information, that her grandparents came from the old country, in order to give Mrs. Kazalski a feeling that she does not feel superior because she is American and that she, too, though more remotely, has a "foreign" background. She uses this opportunity, though it may not have been the next question on the card, to ask how long Mrs. Kazalski has been in America.

Then Mrs. Kazalski's speculations are broken into with a request that startles and frightens her, "Now tell me about the children's work." She is shocked into silence, but already some confidence has been established, and her interest has been aroused. Mrs. Kazalski recognizes by the open, direct way in which the interviewer makes her request that Miss Egmont is not trying to trap her.

"I'd like to know," Miss Egmont went on, in her soft, even voice, "about the work you and the children do in the cannery—just what you do, and how much you earn, and what time you go to work, and some other things. But first, are you sure you understand just why I'm asking these questions? Sometimes people are suspicious, can't understand why the government, far off in Washington, should send someone away down here to ask questions. Maybe you'd like to ask me some questions before you answer mine?"

"Mrs. Oshinsky says you come to collect the fines."

"Fines?"

"The twenty-five dollars for people, if their children work. You inspector?"

"No," said Miss Egmont, simply, and it surprised Mrs. Kazalski that the accusation did not embarrass her. "There are inspectors," Miss Egmont continued, "and there are fines for employing children; but the bosses, not the workers, pay the fines. Only, my work has nothing to do with fines. The government is making a study of what's good for children and what's bad for children. You see, children are the most valuable things in the world; but it is only lately people have learned that in order to make them healthier and happier, we have to study them, and see how things affect them. The Children's Bureau is finding out how work affects them—how it affects their health and their chances of growing up strong and healthy and happy. What do you think about it? How do you feel about the work your children do, and the other children?"

Mrs. Kazalski had never thought of it. But the question turned her scrutiny back from her visitor to herself. It half flashed through her mind that she had never before thought of anything aside from how to get money for the next day's living; how to keep her children and her house clean; what to cook; whether the oysters would be large or small; how to pick out the wettest can and to work quickly, so that as much water as possible could get in with the oyster-meat, before it was weighed.

But now, here was a new thing. Her opinion was being asked. She shrugged her shoulders. What had she to do with these things?

Here Miss Egmont gives a little further explanation and straightforwardly anticipates for Mrs. Kazalski some of the questions that will later be asked. She has sensed Mrs. Kazalski's "hardened face and unwillingness to continue." She expresses her recognition of Mrs. Kazalski's feelings by asking: ". . . Are you sure you understand just why I'm asking these questions? . . . Maybe you'd like to ask me some questions before you answer mine?" This approach again gives Mrs. Kazalski the feeling that she is sharing in the conversation, that Miss Egmont wants to understand her and is not merely routinely pumping her. The wording of this question is more encouraging than, say, a blunt query, such as "Have you any questions?" which might merely discourage elucidation. Through this question Miss Egmont discovers the worry back of the hardness, the fear that the interviewer is there to collect twenty-five dollars. Without this question or a similar one encouraging Mrs. Kazalski to express herself, Miss Egmont might have attempted to conduct the interview without having any clues as to why she was meeting with such stubborn resistance. Now she knows "what is on the other one's mind" and can deal with that fear rather than struggle with the stubbornness that was the external manifestation of it.

In the explanation Miss Egmont gives of the work of the Children's Bureau, instead of assuming dogmatically that it is right and that Mrs. Kazalski should answer questions, she again elicits Mrs. Kazalski's participation by asking her, "What do you think about it?" Mrs. Kazalski is startled and encouraged by having her opinion asked.

Yet something quite strange and new seemed to be pushing up in her mind. A slow anger was part of it, but there was another element in it, too. She had an opinion, and she wanted, not to be silent and sullen with this government lady, but to talk, to argue with her. Presently she was answering:

"I think too bad for children to work; but what you can do? It's better to work and live, than to starve and die. What would do poor people without husband, if the children don't work? Without the children, I no could make half to live on. Even with children, I got a debt eighteen dollars, at the

"Only a Conversation"
93

store. And you—the government—it don't give money, no? No, just questions it gives. How can help us—questions? The row-boss say you get money for questions, that's why things cost too much—for tax. You say it's good for children—questions. Will it help my children?"

This was a long speech for Mrs. Kazalski. She was breathing hard and perspiring with the effort of it.

Miss Egmont's face was thoughtful. "I'm not absolutely sure it will help your children." She spoke slowly, experienced in making simple people understand new things. "I'm not sure the results of a study like this will come soon enough, though they may come in time to help the younger ones. Do you know," she went on, "that some states give money to widows, so that their children can go to school? And that, in some countries, fathers and bosses and the government together pay for insurance, so that, if the father dies, the mother will have some money every month, and won't have to put the children to work? Well, how do you suppose those countries and those states came to do these things? They sent people like me to go and study what the people needed, how they lived and how they worked; and then they planned ways to help them. But it takes time, and to learn these things we must depend on what the workers tell us, and what the bosses tell us. You, when you tell me about your children's work and about your work, are helping the government to make things better for all children, even though the changes may not come tomorrow or for several years. I believe they will come in your children's lifetime. Don't you want to help make things better for children?"

Mrs. Kazalski felt strangely moved. Only partly by the argument of her visitor, only partly by the visitor's personality. Mainly, it was the fact of this visit, the fact of this conversation, which had swerved her mind from its familiar groove into the rough vastness of new thinking. To think, for the first time in one's life, of anything outside the range of one's experience and observation, is a profound experience. As Mrs. Kazalski's untutored but not stupid mind followed Miss Egmont's simple explanation, she forgot about her debt to the store, forgot Katie's cough (for Katie, listening intently, had not coughed for some minutes). A strange emotion welled up in her, a feeling of value, a feeling that her children were really important, not only to herself, but to the country.

The elicitation of Mrs. Kazalski's opinion enables her to release some of her pent-up hostility just as the previous straightforward question as to whether Mrs. Kazalski understood why Miss Egmont was there releases the fear back of her sullenness. The expression of hostility also furthers the progress of the interview, because with its expression Mrs. Kazalski feels some lessening of the tension she has been feeling in repressing her hostility. Furthermore, her account gives Miss Egmont considerable new understanding of the situation.

Mrs. Kazalski's challenge, "Will it help my children?" does not, as it might have, put the interviewer on the defensive. Consequently she is not tempted to reassure Mrs. Kazalski falsely. Instead, she takes Mrs. Kazalski's question seriously and tries to answer it honestly without making glowing promises. Frequently an interviewer, when challenged as to whether he can really help, is impelled by his own uncertainty to offer dogmatic assurances that serve as much to reassure him as the interviewee.

Since Mrs. Kazalski has shown by her willingness to express herself that she now has some confidence in Miss Egmont, the latter feels able to offer a more detailed explanation of her work. She does so, basing her account on what she has learned thus far about Mrs. Kazalski. Using familiar language, she lets her know that she is part of the study and that she can help by talking frankly. Miss Egmont talks about things that Mrs. Kazalski can understand—children, school, jobs—rather than about abstractions such as child labor and democracy. "Don't you want to help make things better for children?" appeals directly to Mrs. Kazalski's own interests. Children are something she knows about. She lives with them and for them every day.

Mrs. Kazalski is moved "only partly by the argument, . . . only partly by the visitor's personality." This statement reflects the difference between intellectual and emotional understanding. She understands the meaning of Miss Egmont's words, but she also senses the feeling behind them, the desire to help. A sense of personal dignity stirs in her a feeling that her ideas are important and that what she can say will be really helpful.

She shook her head several times. "It should be a good work," she said slowly, at last. And when Miss Egmont took up her questioning again, with "How did you happen to leave Baltimore, to come down here?" Mrs. Kazalski found herself wanting to tell the whole story of her hardships. It would be blessed relief to talk about her troubles, to put them into words, to a person quite detached from her life, someone she would never see again. Never had she done this; never had it occurred to her. She had always thought of her burdens as inevitable, inflicted by Providence, goading her to laborious, irksome effort, which offered no reward. She was not a woman to pity herself, but now, as she poured forth her tale, it was as if she had been given the power to stand apart and see herself; and a rush of self-pity, the first she had known, flooded her for the moment—a strange indulgence of pain that was hotter, but softer, than the hard accepting silence of her many months. Yet there was nothing in her voice, no moisture in her eyes, to tell Miss Egmont, who listened with understanding, of her emotion. She had sent the children out of doors, and in a low voice—that her neighbors might not hear—she had begun:

"Things were enough good with us, till the accident. After five months sick, my man dies; and was left in the house only five dollars thirty-eight cents. Katie coughed bad. That night came the row-boss—"

She told of Mike Salinsky's visit, of her trip down, of her disappointment; of the draughty coldness of the canning-shed in bad wet weather; how the roof of her house "leaked like a basket" when it rained; how she lay awake at night, too tired to sleep, worrying, waiting for the siren, yet dreading it; waiting and dreading the watchman's pounding on the door, which never failed to fill her with anger; hating to force the children from their beds at four or five or six o'clock in the morning—according to the size of the catch; how fast the shucking-gloves wore out—"one glove a day, and we cut our hands yet"; how much worse picking shrimps was than shucking oysters, because of the acid in the head of the shrimps: "After two days at shrimps, my hands look like butcher-shop, but that's the only one thing to make think there is in the world meat! And the stink! You smelt it once? So!"

But, worst of all, was the worry about Katie's cough. That kept recurring again and again in her outpouring. She talked with the simple vividness of a person unused to fluent speech. "I no would care about work, I no would care for

"*Only a Conversation*"
97

nothing, if Katie could get well. When I go away from Baltimore, I say, charity the Kazalskis no take. But now I think foolish to be more proud than to care of your child's health. It ain't proud, having them work over mud and wet, in clothes soaked and torn like noodles. And I think maybe oysters no good for the cough."

Mrs. Kazalski is now able to tell her story freely, and as she talks a new idea begins to evolve. "Through talking" it takes on more definite form: " . . . Now I think foolish to be more proud than to care of your child's health."

"Did you ask the boss if he would send you back now, instead of waiting till the end?"

Mrs. Kazalski laughed bitterly. "He gave me a mouthful," she said.

"Excuse me, I tell you all this," she went on, "but you want to know why children got to work. That's why. But if Katie could get well, I'd give—I'd give—well, I ain't got nothing to give. Excuse me, miss, your face looks very sorry. But you ask—and now you know."

Miss Egmont was silent for a while. Then she said, "Did your husband's boss do nothing for you when he died?"

"Why should he do something? It was no his fault—the accident. My man,—" she paused, "—he good worker, nine year one boss; but he make himself the accident. Sixteen hours he work, and he was much tired. He was good worker, but we no could ask something from the boss, when my husband make the accident."

"When you get back to Baltimore, what will you do?"

Mrs. Kazalski had asked herself this same question many times, and never had she found any answer. But now, miraculously, she discovered that she had a plan, a plan that sprang up of its own accord, that rushed forth, almost as a part of her outpouring.

"I go to a charity. I say, 'Let me take money for rooms; I take lodgers, so I can get a doctor for Katie; I take in washings; I pay back the money.' Maybe I pay neighbor to take care the baby; I go to factory, maybe. But I send my children on the school; they should grow up, like you say, like people, not like pigs. What for I leave Baltimore, to come down to this pig-life, I don't know. If only," she added, wistfully, "if only Katie should live till we get back."

Miss Egmont looked away, out of the open doorway, to the Gulf. The water was a deep blue. A white sail moved slowly, in the sunlight, along the horizon.

"Well," she said, bringing her eyes back to Mrs. Kazalski, "you have had a hard time. But there are only six weeks more, and you have been here, you say, nearly fourteen already. Six weeks is not so terribly long. About the debt, I should not worry too much. Are you the only person here with a debt at the store?"

"Oh, no! All people got debt at the store!"

"Well, surely the company won't want to keep all of you here, for your debt. At the worst, they will take some of your bedding to pay for it. And there may be a heavy run of oysters. And thank you very much for giving me this information. Would you mind if I look over this card, to see that I haven't forgotten to ask anything? I'm supposed to have an answer for every question."

Mrs. Kazalski did not accuse her of indifference. Her mind was so occupied with her sudden, new plans for the ordering of her life on her return to Baltimore, that she was scarcely conscious of Miss Egmont.

Miss Egmont stayed a few minutes longer to get in detail the earnings of each member of the family since their

"Only a Conversation"
99

coming, and the hours of work. Presently she left, hoping things would go better, hoping Katie would improve, suggesting a Baltimore clinic.

Mrs. Kazalski's recital concerns recent events, and we may assume that this timeliness is one reason why she is able to obtain so much release from airing her troubles. If her present predicament had been due to more remote causes, this outpouring would have been less effective. Miss Egmont's question, "Did you ask the boss if he would send you back now?" is one that implies a plan; yet it is quite different from, "Why don't you ask the boss if he will send you back?" It suggests a possible procedure without in any way forcing it upon the interviewee. It also leaves Mrs. Kazalski entirely free to make her own plans.

The interviewer's next question about workmen's compensation is for information. Then, "When you get back to Baltimore, what will you do?" is a question to stimulate Mrs. Kazalski into making a plan for herself. It is practical and realistic, in contrast to the emotional recital of Mrs. Kazalski's recent experiences. It serves to channel Mrs. Kazalski's aroused feeling into practical planning. In answer to this question Mrs. Kazalski "miraculously" discovers that she has a plan.

Some may be inclined to dismiss this illustration because it is fiction, because in real life it could not have happened this way. But experience indicates that such "miracles" are not uncommon. The interviewer was wise in letting the plan come from Mrs. Kazalski. Had she proposed one to her, it would not have been accepted with the conviction and emotional support of one that was self-originated.

Then, with some reassurance about the debt, Miss Egmont winds up the interview on a more practical note, returning to the details of filling in her card. Just as it is unwise to plunge quickly into an interview, so it is always unwise, if the content of an interview has been rather emotional, to end it too abruptly. It is best to take some time before leaving to discuss more matter-of-fact details so as not to leave the person in a highly emotional state.

Mrs. Kazalski went back to her washtub. She could hear Miss Egmont making the same explanation in the next compartment, could hear her neighbor's guarded, reluctant answers. She did not listen to the words, though she could easily have heard them—at first. But after a while her neighbor's voice lowered. Then it occurred to her that perhaps her neighbor had some trouble as real as her own; perhaps—why, surely every woman in the camp had troubles. Most of them were widows, most of them had children to support. And perhaps other women, all over the country! Why, of course, it was right that the government should send someone down to see how things were!

That night she went to bed with a new feeling. It was as if, for the first time in her life, she was fully alive. Not happy, but awake. Sometimes, in her youth,—say, fourteen years ago,—at a wedding in Galicia, after a peasant dance, she had a feeling akin to this, yet different. Then the dancing made one forget the hard furrows and the heavy plough. Now there was no forgetting, rather a full remembering, a coming alive of her mind. A full remembering of herself, and, therefore, of others.

Yet, she told herself, nothing had happened, really. A woman had come, had asked questions, had gone away. She had answered questions, had stated her situation. "Yet nothing has happened," she repeated to herself in Polish, "only a conversation. Talk, only." The debt was still unpaid, Katie was this minute coughing, and life in Baltimore, at the end of six weeks, would be a hard struggle, even though she now had a plan. Why then this new courage, this strange, warm feeling, which reached out, even beyond this roomful of her own family—which included even more than the whole camp? Was this, she asked herself, what they meant by patriotism?

The wind blew, and the single palm tree outside her door crackled. The sound was like the rattle of hard rain. Other nights she had hated it, had thought it mournful, but now she liked it. She raised her head from the bed, and through the window she could see the tree. The moonlight seemed to drip off the sharp fingers of the leaves. Splotches of light and black shadows made a grotesquery; and for the first time she saw a beauty in it. She could close her ears to the heavy breathing of her neighbors, and to Katie's cough, and could listen to the orchestra of crickets and frogs, against the night's outer silence, with—was it possible?—almost with happiness.

Perhaps the outstanding quality of this interview is the skill revealed in getting a reluctant person to talk. The change from "No gov'ment lady or man neither won't get something out of me" to the free outpourings of Mrs. Kazalski's story is remarkable.

One might well question the wisdom of letting Mrs. Kazalski tell so much when this interview was known to be a single contact and when the interviewer was not in a position to do anything about Mrs. Kazalski's grievances. She has to gather up her cards, fill in a few more blank spaces, and move on to the next of several hundred women in the camp. One is justified in speculating about the extent to which, under such circumstances, an interviewer should let the interview proceed. Many of the women in the camp undoubtedly had similar difficulties, and we may well question whether "only a conversation" would be equally effective in every case. Is there not perhaps more likelihood that such a procedure would stir up rather than resolve anxieties?

An important consideration is the fact that, although the interview stirs up a good deal of feeling, it is feeling centered largely around recent and current experiences. Actually, the interviewer does not go into Mrs. Kazalski's past or attempt to get at deeper motivations. Another safeguard in this interview is the very fact that both interviewer and interviewee know in advance that this interview is to be a single contact. Mrs. Kazalski is not led to believe that she will continue to see Miss Egmont and get further help from her. The interviewer's limited purpose in talking with her is stated clearly throughout, thus tying the interview to a known firm basis.

It should not be concluded that the sort of catharsis provided here by "only a conversation" would always be so effective. If Mrs. Kazalski's present dilemma was only one link in a long chain of disastrous experiences, she would probably have gotten no release from thus unburdening herself.

The interview does show, however, that when the circumstances are favorable, a skilled interviewer can render invaluable service in the course of the interview itself.

9

"You're Not Obligated to Me Like a Brother Is"

Although handled by a professional Travelers Aid Society worker, the following case illustrates the kind of skillful help that could be given by a sensitive, well-trained casework assistant or volunteer—a person who has learned how to meet the practical and emotional needs of people who require assistance in coping with an emergency situation. These interviews were selected because the principles they demonstrate can be applied in many settings other than a social work agency. Whenever a person is facing a critical situation alone—if he is ill, or old, or uncertain of what the future holds for him even in such ordinary matters as where to live—he needs the reassurance that someone cares about him, that someone will provide concrete evidence of interest in his welfare and the necessary emotional support to sustain him as he takes the steps toward his future. A nurse in a hospital ward meeting a new patient, an admissions clerk in an institution, and a staff assistant in a rehabilitation clinic are only a few examples of persons who daily encounter situations similar to that faced by Eric Rasmussen.

[The Travelers Aid Society office in an eastern city was notified on December 28 by an airline clerk that an elderly man who seemed frail and ill needed assistance in continuing his trip to St. Louis. He was brought from the airport to the TAS office in the city, and then, because it was evening, the TAS worker arranged for him to be taken to a hotel. She promised that another worker would see him the following day to help him work out plans. Mr. Rasmussen volunteered that he was sixty-seven years old and believed that he had multiple sclerosis. He had been born in Denmark and had come to the United States with a brother forty-five years before. He and his brother had settled in St. Louis, where he had worked as a mechanic. He had three brothers and three sisters still living in Denmark, and over the years he had made several visits to see them. He maintained himself on a pension and Social Security benefits.

A year earlier, Mr. Rasmussen had returned to Denmark, planning to stay there permanently. He had not, however, enrolled in the Danish medical insurance plan; and when he became ill, his relatives decided it would be better for him to return to the United States, where he would be eligible for free medical care. He had written to his brother Leif in St. Louis, who had answered, "Stay there." His brothers and sisters in Denmark, however, had not agreed and had arranged for him to return by plane.

Mr. Rasmussen revealed that he had $1,000 sewn into his underwear. He understood that TAS would get in touch with his brother to arrange for his return to St. Louis.

The next morning the worker was given the above information and telephoned Mr. Rasmussen.]

"You're Not Obligated to Me Like a Brother Is"

I introduced myself and asked, "How are you?" Mr. Rasmussen replied, in a voice that I thought was slow and shaky, that he was fine, that he had been able to get up and dress, and that he had had his breakfast brought to his room. Since finishing his meal, he had been lying down. I said I would be coming to see him, but I wanted to know whether there was anything he needed or wanted to talk about before I came. He said he was concerned about keeping his room for another night and asked whether I could help with this matter. I agreed to notify the reservation desk for him and told him our office in St. Louis would try to talk to his brother that day.

I asked whether he had anything to read, and when he said, "No," I offered to bring a newspaper or magazines. When I asked whether he had a television set, he said he had one but did not know how to turn it on. I suggested he call the desk clerk and ask that someone come to his room and show him how to operate the set.

I called Mr. Rasmussen again before leaving the office to let him know when to expect me. He said he was not feeling well and described a lameness and unsteady feeling that came and went. He had not seen a doctor since becoming ill in Denmark, and he was not taking any medication. I asked again if I could bring him anything, and he responded, "Coffee and custard pie, please—and a newspaper." He added that he would give me the name and address of a friend in St. Louis when I came.

Even before the worker meets Mr. Rasmussen, she has established a beginning relationship with him by her demonstration of interest in his situation and concern about his welfare. This concern must have been welcomed by a man who had so recently experienced rejection by his relatives abroad and his brother in this country. When, in a second telephone call, he is asked what he would like, he is able to make a request. To a man who for the last several months seemingly has not been consulted about his wishes, but has had the management of his affairs taken out of his hands and who because of poor health feels he has to be dependent, it is a happy change to find that someone is consulting him about what he wants and needs.

When I arrived at the hotel, I telephoned Mr. Rasmussen from the lobby, and he gave me his room number. He was sick looking, fragile, and thin and had the appearance of a man in his eighties. He moved very slowly, and his hands shook. He spoke in a logical way, seemed to have a good memory, and showed no evidence of time or place disorientation.

Because of his difficulty in moving around, I arranged the pie and coffee for him. It was so hot and musty in the room that I asked if I might open the window. He agreed but asked me to remember to close it before I left because he was afraid of a draft. He then went on to repeat most of what he had told the TAS worker the night before. He said his brother had a daughter living outside St. Louis, but he could not remember her married name. He had never met her husband. He thought his brother might be visiting her during this holiday weekend. I asked about other persons who might be able to meet him if we could not locate his brother, and he gave me the name of a friend, an elderly single man. He also had some cousins, but they were in their eighties, and he did not want them to be bothered about him.

I asked about his health, and he said that the Danish doctor who had vaccinated him had told him he "probably" had multiple sclerosis. Years before he had had blood poisoning in his left leg, which pained him in cold weather. The previous winter was the first winter, however, that he sometimes could not walk on the leg. The weakness seemed to have spread slowly to his right side. I expressed sympathy and asked how he had managed the flight, knowing he had been brought to the TAS office in a wheelchair. He said that was the first time he had used one; the previous winter he had used only a cane.

I asked what I could do for him. He said he wanted to pay the hotel, and he gave me $50. He told me to be sure to ask for a receipt. Because I thought he might be worried about my going off with his money, I said I would leave my coat on the chair while I went downstairs. His room cost $13.34. I counted out the change for him when I came back. He had trouble getting his wallet out of his pocket, and it took him a long time to put the bills away, even with some help from me.

Because he seemed so frail, I began to discuss possible alternatives, such as going to a hospital or seeing a doctor locally. He was firm about wanting to proceed to St. Louis and enter a hospital there. He did not want to see a local doctor or go to a hospital before returning to St. Louis because he "might have to stay too long." I said I guessed that perhaps he was afraid he could not leave the hospital. He nodded agreement. He wanted to get a hotel room in St. Louis and then go into a hospital. He asked me about paying for the hospital, and I explained about Medicare and Medicaid. I suggested that he might be able to leave his suitcase with his brother or take it to the hospital with him. He thought this idea was a good one, to save him the expense of renting a hotel room. I reminded him that we had to wait to hear from our St. Louis office before we could make definite plans.

I asked whether he had turned on the television. He had not, although he had been told how to do it. I said, "People can get lonely when they stay in one room." He replied, "Especially when it's so small." I said it was nice to hear voices and suggested he turn on the TV. Because I was sitting next to it, he repeated the directions to me. I then asked him to try it and helped him until he could turn the set on by himself.

Mr. Rasmussen told me he had eaten eggs for breakfast, but he preferred oatmeal. I suggested he order it the next day. He nodded and complained of being constipated. He said he did not want to take any medicine because it made his whole body feel terrible. I suggested prunes. He nodded again and said he had some fig juice in a bottle. I said I would call at ten the next morning to make sure he got up. He took a clock from his suitcase and asked me to set it. Since he had said he was not ordering dinner, I asked him whether it was because he thought the breakfast had been too expensive. He thought it was moderate for a hotel like this one, but he could get food cheaper. Because I felt he was worried about spending his money, I offered to bring soup when I visited the next day.

While I was putting on my coat, Mr. Rasmussen said to me, "You are not obligated to me like a brother is—a brother is financially and otherwise obligated." I agreed that what he said was true—a brother did have a different obligation—but I said I would visit him daily while he was in the city. I assured him that he would not be left alone and that I would work with him to get him settled. He seemed reassured and smiled.

Observing Mr. Rasmussen's frailty and impaired ability to move easily, the worker unobtrusively helps him by arranging the food, opening a window, paying the hotel bill, and demonstrating how to turn on the television set. She does not, however, make the mistake of assuming that he is a completely helpless person. Whenever possible, she encourages him to do for himself and thereby demonstrates more effectively than words could her recognition that, despite his illness, he is still capable of some self-direction. Her genuine interest in the details of his present situation must have been heartwarming to a sick, elderly man in an unfamiliar city, dependent on strangers for help in returning to a brother who he knows does not want him. But his visitor evidently does not seem to Mr. Rasmussen to be a complete stranger. He has talked with her on the telephone before meeting her; he has made a request for food and a newspaper, which she brings; and her questions make him feel she is concerned about his health and understands how lonely one can be shut up in a hotel room. Although Mr. Rasmussen's response of volunteering information indicates his trust in the worker, she is aware that he has just met her; when she takes the fifty dollars, she visibly reassures him of her return by leaving her coat in his room while she goes to the lobby.

The worker's sensitivity is further apparent in the discussion of alternate plans when she recognizes his fear of permanent hospitalization. Mr. Rasmussen is not unaware of her empathy. He may have been comparing her kind and understanding attitude with that of his relatives when he comments, "You're not obligated to me like a brother is. . . ." The worker does not describe his tone of voice as incredulous, but it may have been. In a sense he has been abandoned by his relatives, and he has little reason to think his welfare is of concern to anyone except perhaps the one friend he mentioned. The worker's assurance that his welfare is of concern to her and that she will visit him daily and help him get settled brings forth a smile of relief and appreciation from Mr. Rasmussen.

[Later that day the TAS worker in St. Louis reported that Leif Rasmussen had agreed, reluctantly, to meet his brother and drive him to a temporary lodging place, but he could do nothing further for him. The worker had arranged for a room in a nursing home and had made an appointment for Mr. Rasmussen to see a caseworker in an agency for the aged the following week.]

I telephoned Mr. Rasmussen to tell him that a reservation had been made for him on an afternoon flight to St. Louis on December 31. He agreed to the time, to going to the nursing home for a few days, and to having a medical checkup in the nursing home. He also wanted to keep the appointment at the agency for the aged. He was concerned, however, about his limited financial resources.

The next day, December 30, I confirmed the plane reservation, the reservation at the nursing home, and the appointment at the agency for the aged. I requested a wheelchair at the local airport and similar assistance for Mr. Rasmussen on his arrival in St. Louis. Later I telephoned Mr. Rasmussen again to tell him when to expect me and to ask what kind of soup he wanted.

While he was eating his soup, I went over all the details of his trip and gave him a written schedule. He said he knew of the nursing home, but he was "worried about getting out to the airport." I said I would accompany him if he wanted me to do so. "Yes," Mr. Rasmussen replied, "I want you to come with me." When I told him about having reserved a wheelchair for him, he said that except for coming to the TAS office, he had never used one. I commented that because it would be New Year's Eve, I thought the airport would be crowded, with people pushing and shoving, and the wheelchair would make it easier for him to manage in a crowd. I asked whether he minded using one. Although he said no, I thought he was reluctant and added that we could decide after we got to the airport.

I reminded him that the day before we had planned for him to get out of his room for a short time. I suggested that we go to the lobby and chat for a while because our "business" was completed for the day. He gave me the money for his room and plane fare and asked me to help him put on his coat. Then he asked me to stay in the room while he tried to open the door from the outside. Because the barrel of the lock was loose, he had difficulty. Although I tried to help him with verbal instructions, he could manage to unlock the door only once and decided he was "forced" to stay in his room. On our way to the elevator, I noticed that he walked slowly and had trouble turning corners.

When we sat down in the lobby, the manager offered Mr. Rasmussen a cane, which he refused. During our chat he told me about his avocation as a violinist and of his travels with a group of musicians for over twenty years. He had seen Canada and a good part of the United States. He could no longer play the violin. He asked my age and where I came from, and he wanted to know about my family. We shared some life experiences. When I suggested we return to his room, he said, "Please, let's stay a little longer." We remained in the lobby and chatted another fifteen minutes. I went back to his room with him, reminded him of the written schedule, and said I would call at 10:00 A.M. the next day and would be at the hotel at 12:30 P.M.

In the second interview we see the careful preparation the worker is giving Mr. Rasmussen for his flight the following day. Her consistent attention to details is reassuring to Mr. Rasmussen, and he agrees to the plans being made for him because he has been consulted and kept fully informed. When he seems reluctant to accept the use of a wheelchair, he is told the decision can be made when he reaches the airport. He is given an explanation that does not emphasize his poor physical condition, but rather the hectic conditions in an airport during the holidays. The effort involved for him in the short trip to the lobby indicates the wisdom of the worker's suggestion that he consider using a wheelchair. Mr. Rasmussen's wish to manage without such aids is further evidenced in his refusal of the cane offered by the hotel manager. But he does admit to a need for support when he indirectly asks for help in getting to the airport. The worker's ready offer of escort service—a service of her agency—is made after his expression of worry about how he will manage. The offer could have been made earlier, but the worker's sensitivity to Mr. Rasmussen's desire to be in control of his affairs leads her to wait for an indication from him.

It is interesting to speculate on why the worker suggested the "social chat" in the lobby. She did not record her discussion of it with Mr. Rasmussen, but it seems likely that she wanted to relieve the monotony and the isolation he felt in the small hotel room and to offer him some friendly companionship in addition to the help with his problems. She makes the distinction for him when she points out that they have completed their business. Mr. Rasmussen responds by telling her stories of his life in happier years, and he expresses interest in her life. "We shared some life experiences" is indicative of a natural, warm response of one human being to another, one that has meaning to each, no matter how brief their encounter.

It is important to note that instances when social conversation with clients is appropriate are the exception rather than the rule. In this situation the worker planned to lighten the boredom and the resultant strain on an elderly man temporarily confined in a hotel, to help him regain some self-esteem and feeling that he was a part of society by her readiness to "just talk" with him. Mr. Rasmussen can differentiate between the discussion of his problems and a friendly conversation in a lobby. The respite it affords him is shown in his request to "stay a little longer," to which the worker accedes. Mr. Rasmussen is not facing a happy future, but he can respond to the opportunity to talk of other matters, to learn some facts about his newly acquired friend, and in the discussion to reveal himself as the personable man he is.

The next morning I telephoned Mr. Rasmussen and then went to his hotel at 12:30 P.M. with coffee for both of us. We discussed the plan to get to the airport and tipping— whom and how much. In the taxi he again expressed concern about the cost of the nursing home and asked whether he could stay in an inexpensive hotel instead. I said he might be able to get a hotel room after he got to St. Louis, but because of the holidays it might be better for him to stay in the nursing home for the weekend. After further discussion, he agreed to the nursing home but thought he would talk to his brother and the Travelers Aid worker about another place.

When we reached the airport, I asked for a wheelchair, and Mr. Rasmussen, after he got into it, commented: "It's a good idea. The walk to the gate is very long." While we waited, Mr. Rasmussen reviewed the details of boarding the plane, showing his ticket, and taking off his coat. He asked what I would do when I left the airport and whether I would know what happened to him. I assured him I would hear from the Travelers Aid worker in St. Louis.

The airline steward told me to accompany Mr. Ras-mussen to the plane, but we were stopped en route by the stewardess, who said she would see him onto the plane. Our farewell, therefore, was rather abrupt. I waited by the window for several minutes in case Mr. Rasmussen was seated where he could see me.

On Mr. Rasmussen's last day in the city, the worker again is prompt in telephoning him and arriving at the hotel to escort him to the airport. Her promptness alleviates undue anxiety on his part, and her bringing coffee for both of them is another evidence of her friendly interest.

With the careful advance preparation, the trip to the airport goes smoothly. The worker's decision to ask for a wheelchair is approved by her client when he sees the long distance he would have to walk. He reveals how much the relationship means to him when he asks what she plans to do after he leaves and whether she will know what happens to him. She assures him that she will hear from the worker whom he will meet in St. Louis.

The leave-taking was unexpectedly hurried, and one senses the worker's disappointment that it was abrupt. With her customary sensitivity she reacts with concern for Mr. Rasmussen. If the farewell was sudden to her, perhaps it could feel like a desertion to a man as alone as he. She does the only thing she can do now to reassure him: she waits for several minutes hoping he may be able to see her and know she continues to be interested in him.

10

"I Don't Want Any Want Any Hassles"

Often it is hard for an adolescent to ask for help and to talk with an adult in an established agency. An adolescent is trying to become independent, to separate himself from his family, to feel secure as a young adult. The need for help stirs up his fear of again becoming babyish and dependent as well as his fear of not being capable of handling a problem alone. Thus, an adolescent may present a mélange of contradictory demands and rapidly shifting moods. An interviewer has to be especially sensitive to unspoken needs beneath the voiced request and attuned to feelings while remaining a steady advocate of what is feasible.

The following series of interviews illustrates a worker's skill in maintaining a supportive, nonpunitive attitude despite the adolescent's anger and outright hostility. The setting is the social service department of a large hospital in a state in which the law has recently been changed to permit therapeutic abortion under specified circumstances and according to a new set of procedures.

Cindy, a pretty eighteen-year-old, was dressed in the fashion typical of the teen-age culture. She had been directed to the social service department after a hospital laboratory test had confirmed that she was pregnant.

From the very outset of the interview, Cindy's manner was hostile. She perched rigidly on the edge of the chair as if to be ready for flight. Her face was hidden by her long, straight hair; she looked at the floor and twisted her rings. She said she had come because she had heard we could tell her how to get a therapeutic abortion. I said, "We certainly can discuss that as one of the possible solutions." She looked up sharply and said angrily: "I don't want any hassles! If you can't help me get an abortion, I'll go somewhere else." She went on to say that she had done all the thinking she needed to do and that abortion was the only possible solution. If I was not going to help her, she might as well leave; she and her boyfriend would find a way to get her an abortion one way or another.

I said it sounded as if she must have had some anxious moments after she first suspected that she was pregnant. Could she tell me a little about what she and her boyfriend had discussed as possibilities? Angrily and impatiently she said they did not have many choices: marriage was out, and she was in no position to bring up a baby alone. She fell silent, and I waited a few moments before I gently asked whether she had thought of the possibility of placing the baby for adoption. Her eyes flashing, she burst out that giving your baby away was the cruelest thing she could imagine.

"Anyone who can even consider doing such a thing is sick!"
I said I could see that she had many strong feelings about
her situation and that she was not having an easy time. She
lowered her head despondently but made no reply.

I asked whether she could tell me a little about herself,
but she merely shrugged her shoulders and looked away in
disgust. She was reluctant to answer even simple, factual
questions and sulkily gave terse, noncommital answers. I
asked whether she understood why I had to ask these questions and commented that she sounded so unhappy about
answering them. She shook her head and mumbled something
about not seeing why she had to "go through all this." I told
her I realized my questions made her impatient and that they
might even make it seem as if I was trying to put her off.
However, I really needed to get some idea of what she and
her life were like in order to know what suggestions might
be most helpful to her.

Though still sullen and hostile, Cindy gradually began
to talk a little about herself. By following her cues I learned
that she was the youngest of three children—two boys and
a girl—born to parents who had been divorced shortly after
her birth. After the divorce her mother had gone to work
and had sent Cindy to live with her maternal grandparents
and an unmarried aunt. The two boys, who were of school
age, had remained with her mother. Even when her mother's
situation had eased somewhat, Cindy had continued to live
with her grandparents and aunt, whom she described as both
overindulgent and inflexibly strict. The previous year her
grandmother had died, and her grandfather and aunt had
moved to another state. Cindy had then gone to live with
her recently remarried mother and her stepfather.

I asked how this arrangement had worked out. She said
she did not get along too badly with her mother. Her mother,

however, had a full-time job and spent a great deal of her free time with her new husband, who was "quite a good guy." She sighed and said that she missed her grandmother even though she had been a real square and very strict. She still felt like an only child, since both brothers were away from home. Although she did not articulate it, a sense of isolation and loneliness was apparent in the way she talked of her living situation; I also sensed that she felt like an unintentional intruder in the lives of her mother and step-father.

Cindy had just completed her freshman year at a local college and was then working at a summer job. She spoke with enthusiasm only when discussing her boyfriend, whom she had dated for several years. She talked of him and of his large, casual family with real warmth. I commented on her feeling for him, and she said that Johnny was a wonderful person and that they planned to marry when he finished college. She added quickly that they had talked a great deal about her pregnancy and knew that abortion was the only answer.

I asked Cindy what she knew about the procedure for determining eligibility for a therapeutic abortion. She was almost totally uninformed and naive about the whole process. When I spelled out for her what was involved, she became quite angry, saying: "You mean I have to go through all that and then may be turned down? If I'd known all that, I'd never have come." I said I realized that having to wait for a decision was not easy and that many women I had talked with found it hard to accept the fact that they would have to go over the same ground with a psychiatrist and an obstetrician, but that was what the law currently required. I asked whether she had discussed her plans and wishes with her mother. Vehemently she said that her mother knew nothing about her pregnancy and was not going to. When I asked why she was so adamant about her mother's not knowing, she could say nothing beyond the assertion that she would get rid of the baby her own way rather than tell her mother. I said matter-of-factly but gently that there was an additional reality: because she was under twenty-one years of age, parental permission would have to be given for her to receive ongoing medical care. Again she became agitated and angry, saying that her mother had no business interfering in her life as if she were a child. I tried quietly to elaborate on the reality that parental permission to administer anaesthesia was required, but it seemed clear that Cindy was too filled with anxiety to be able to absorb the reality as anything but a personal assault on her supposed autonomy.

I said: "Why don't we do this? Why don't I go ahead and make the appointments you need with the obstetrician and the psychiatrist? The important thing is for you to get good medical care. You and the doctor can then discuss the issue of parental permission." I reminded her that it was not my function to make the decision, but rather to get her to doctors I felt could be most helpful to her. I asked her to stop by to see me several days later so that I could tell her about the appointment times. I also suggested that she call me before then if she was worried.

Two days later Cindy phoned to ask me how she could avoid the nausea that was making her miserable in the morning. I suggested she try munching saltines and told her that the obstetrician would be able to give her more precise professional advice.

Cindy's hiding her face and twisting her rings make the worker suspect that uncertainty and fear are the feelings that lie behind her imperious demand for an abortion. The worker's first response, "We certainly can discuss that [therapeutic abortion] as one of the possible solutions," is an attempt to show receptivity to Cindy's wishes while leaving the door open to other choices. But because Cindy has not had time to know from experience that the worker is concerned about her and wants to be helpful, she reacts with anger, as if the worker were withholding the only assistance that could help her. Cindy's fierce response to the worker's premature suggestion of adoption makes clear that the suggestion has touched on some wellspring of intense feeling.

The worker then takes a different direction, speaking to the girl's unexpressed distress. One senses a slowing of the pace of the interview as the worker backs away from the specific problem of pregnancy and takes some time to get to know the client. In this situation, as in many interviews, what appears to be a long way round may in fact be the most direct route to solving the problem. The worker refuses to be put off by Cindy's resistance. Instead, she acknowledges to Cindy the annoying aspects of agency routines. At the same time, by explaining the purpose of the questions, she appeals to the more grown-up side of Cindy's wish for help. In the context of being an active participant in problem solving, Cindy is able to give information about herself that provides the worker with more understanding of the particular circumstances in Cindy's life that might be influencing her feelings about pregnancy, motherhood, and family ties.

When the worker asks Cindy what she knows about therapeutic abortion before she goes on to explain it, she gives Cindy a chance to prepare herself to hear the realities. The worker understands Cindy's angry remarks as expressions of panic and frustration and responds only to the feelings underneath while implying that both worker and client must seek a solution within the limits of what is realistically available.

The final assault on Cindy's wish to control her destiny

is the necessity for her mother to know about the pregnancy and become involved in what is to be done about it. Again the worker is tempted to stand firm on the rules but realizes that Cindy is as yet unable to listen.

At this point the worker does two things to reinforce the trust Cindy has just begun to place in her. First, she quickly proffers a concrete gift in the form of making necessary next-step appointments, indicating her sincerity about wanting to act in the girl's behalf. Second, she asks Cindy to return in a few days to get details of the appointments and also to keep in touch in the meantime. By doing these things, she gives Cindy a chance to digest what she has heard, to reflect, and to marshal her coping powers.

Cindy's telephone call a few days later to ask for advice about morning sickness makes it abundantly clear that she wants to accept some help, although she does not make a direct request for it.

On the specified day, Cindy returned to find out about her appointments. In contrast to her earlier manner, she seemed much more a frightened, bewildered teen-ager than a strictly go-it-alone girl. She timidly asked what the obstetrician would do to her and admitted that she had never had an internal examination but had heard it was "awful." I told her a little about what the examination would entail and assured her that Dr. Prentiss was kind and gentle. She said she was "scared about what would happen to her insides" if she had an abortion—the thought of it "freaked her out." I said that she would be talking with Dr. Prentiss about the abortion but that the whole point of the careful evaluation was to make sure she was given the most helpful and appropriate advice. I told her that I had mentioned to Dr. Prentiss her reluctance to talk with her mother. Dr. Prentiss would explain why it was necessary to involve her in the situation; either he or I would be glad to talk with her mother and also to help Cindy think about how she might talk to her herself. I said that my concern was for Cindy's unhappiness and that I wished she could realize that she did not have to go through this rough time all by herself. I suggested that she might be feeling worse about herself than she needed to and that perhaps this feeling was what made it hard to talk to her mother. She shook her head and said she had been "just so stupid." I asked whether she thought her mother would think her stupid. Her eyes filled with tears, and she said she thought her mother would be terribly disappointed in her. I said I thought it would be unreasonable to think it would be any easier for her mother to hear about her pregnancy than for her to tell her about it. It is true that her mother might regard it as an error in judgment but not as a negation of Cindy's other attributes and accomplishments, such as her successful completion of a year in college, and the fact that, as she described it, her relationship with Johnny was a very genuine one, with mutual concern and warmth. Cindy listened but made little response. I asked her to please keep in touch, to let me know how things went.

Since Cindy has earlier indicated her desire to have help, the worker is not surprised that in the second interview Cindy can let the worker see that she is scared not only about the unfamiliar medical procedures but also about the possibility of her mother's being disappointed and critical. Without minimizing the problems or being unrealistic, the worker is warm and reassuring about procedures and about parental feelings. The worker has assumed that Cindy, in accusing herself of being "stupid," is afraid that her mother, too, will view her as "stupid." Cindy does indeed dread her mother's response, but she listens to the worker's attempt to explain that a mother might feel distressed but still have affection and appreciation for her daughter.

A few days later, Cindy had her psychiatric interview. Immediately after it, she came flying into my office, expressing a good deal of anger. She said the doctor had no business asking her probing questions about her feelings about abortion. He had gotten her all upset, especially because he had seriously questioned the advisability of abortion and had expressed doubt that it was what she herself really wanted. With energetic scorn, she said, "He said I have mixed feelings!" Outraged, she declared emphatically that it was just not so; she knew what she wanted and was determined to get it. I listened calmly to her protests, finally saying that I knew how difficult it was to be sure you wanted something so badly, then to have to look to others to get it for you, and then to face opposition. I also stated strongly that professional people had the responsibility to make recommendations they felt were in the best interests of a particular patient. Hard as it may seem to believe, what a patient most wanted was not always what was best for him, and it would be a sort of cop-out for a doctor to fail to give a patient the benefit of his own expert assessment.

Cindy listened intently and seemed almost reassured by this firmness. At the same time she forcefully expressed the wish for a guarantee that Dr. Prentiss would be "on her side." She pressed so hard that again I was struck by the amount of energy she was using to maintain her denial of ambivalence. I said that she knew I was very much concerned about how she felt and that I could understand a range of feelings. I knew that at least some part of her wished for a quick and easy resolution to her pregnancy, but the truth was that none of the possible outcomes could be either quick or easy, and I honestly had no way of knowing what Dr. Prentiss's advice to her would be. Once more I expressed a wish to be in touch with her during this painful period.

By the time Cindy's anger is again mobilized by a probing psychiatric interview, her relationship with the worker is secure enough for her to fly to the worker as an ally. Remembering Cindy's love for her firm grandmother and thinking of the adolescent need for clear acknowledgment of what is real, the worker reminds Cindy of the doctor's responsibility not to "cop out" [the adolescent's own lingo] by failing to give his honest opinion. The worker continues to leave open to Cindy the possibility that her feelings about abortion may be more mixed than she has expressed. But she does not confront or challenge Cindy directly.

Several days later I had a call from Cindy asking whether she and her mother could see me before Cindy's appointment with Dr. Prentiss. They came together and I interviewed them together. Cindy appeared more relaxed than I had yet seen her. Her mother seemed slightly uncomfortable, but the primary feeling was one of warm concern for her daughter. Cindy said that she and Johnny had decided that both families had to be told of their predicament. To Cindy's surprise, both sets of parents had been sympathetic in spite of their being upset. Their concern was focused chiefly on Cindy's well-being and on Johnny's and Cindy's future lives. I told the mother that Cindy and I had talked about how difficult it would be to tell her of the pregnancy, but that I had been confident that, of all the complicated feelings brought to the surface, the uppermost would be concern for a troubled Cindy and Johnny. I added that it took the equally admirable strengths of both generations to get together to cope with a tough situation. Cindy said that after her interview with the psychiatrist, and in anticipation of the gynecological examination, she had begun to realize that the idea of "getting rid of our baby" really bothered her, especially since Johnny was acting more "domestic" and she felt increased "tenderness" in their relationship. Looking at both Cindy and her mother, I asked, "What are you thinking of now?" Cindy's mother spoke first and said she was primarily concerned with Cindy's getting good medical advice about her general and prenatal health before any decision could be made. She said that both families, as well as Cindy and Johnny, were seriously considering the possibility of marriage, with the knowledge that if marriage was a reasonable option, family support would be needed to help Johnny finish college. She expressed her belief that both young people could manage and that the families liked each other. She said that the marriage would be sooner than she had expected, but she had confidence in the strength of Cindy and Johnny's relationship.

I said that Cindy and I had talked about the fact that no solution would be an easy one and that such an early marriage could offer problems too, especially if a child was expected so soon. Cindy quickly said that she was sure that she and Johnny would have no problems. I said that "having problems" did not have a critical connotation; that any major decision or adjustment could make for troublesome times; and that my uppermost wish was that whatever the doctors advised and whatever she, her family, and Johnny decided the future would hold, Cindy could value herself enough to avail herself of the support to which she was entitled. I said I would like to help Cindy and her mother in any way possible, both in the present crisis and in the future. Both agreed to get in touch with me following the appointment with Dr. Prentiss, to let me know what was decided.

There is no way of knowing how Cindy arrived at the decision to tell her mother. Perhaps, however, the worker had given her an experience of depending on an adult without feeling held back from maturing. This experience then freed her to turn to her mother.

Conspicuous in the third interview is the worker's attempt to bridge the distance between the generations rather than to deny that such a separation exists. She brings them together by directing her attention toward both mother and daughter, by expressing appreciation of the mother's concern for her daughter's well-being, and by verbalizing her expectation that both generations will bring strengths to bear on working out this problem.

This interview illustrates also the importance of an interviewer's maintaining a nonjudgmental stance and avoiding imposing his own solutions in a situation that can bring forth many contradictory attitudes. A warm but neutral receptivity as the client sorts out his options is likely to be the most effective response for encouraging a client to find his own solutions. In this interview the worker expresses her awareness that no solution is simple and that, whatever course of action is chosen, there are likely to be problems. She is careful to leave the door open so that Cindy and her mother can turn to her later, despite their immediate declaration that all will be well in the future.

11

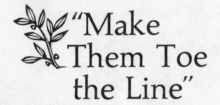 "Make
Them Toe
the Line"

The interviewer's skill in shifting an individual's interest from a job for which he is unfit to one more suited to his personality and abilities is illustrated in the following interview.

Mr. Robertson came to the office of the neighborhood Community Action Program to apply for work assignment. He entered the interviewing room with a rapid, precise stride and then handed me his filled-out application form. As he did so, he remarked that because some of the questions were not worded very clearly, he felt somewhat handicapped in setting down his information. He lit a cigarette and leaned back comfortably in his chair while I scanned his application. I noticed that he was sixty years of age, although he looked no more than fifty. Under employment history I saw that he had changed jobs frequently. Among the different positions he had held were those of clerk, accountant, and floorwalker. While I was looking at the application, his eyes were scrutinizing the room, taking in every detail.

Mr. Robertson had stated his first job preference to be that of auxiliary police patrolman and had specified no second or third choice. I therefore began the interview by asking him why he wished to have this particular type of assignment. His answer was serious and intent. He realized how important it was for all citizens to cooperate and "toe the line" to prevent urban neighborhoods from going downhill and becoming "jungles." He said he would like to see to it that there would be "100 percent cooperation" in the district assigned to him. He had been talking to some of his neighbors recently about what the city might be asking them to do to help with urban renewal and rehabilitation, and the neighbors had not taken the matter very seriously. Some had even said that they would not like to see "anybody bossing them around about their property." Their attitude had irritated him considerably, and he had apparently given them a lecture on good citizenship.

At this point he leaned across the desk confidentially and said he would not be surprised if a couple of families in his neighborhood were "Commies." "They are always making remarks about the government, and sometimes I wonder how far they should be trusted." He asked whether I thought he should turn in their names to us so that we could "report them." I explained that handling such reports was not a part of our job and that, if he felt he had any real complaints about his neighbors, he ought to talk with one of the men in the legal section of the Community Action Program, who might be able to suggest the next move. This suggestion did

"Make Them Toe the Line"
129

not satisfy him entirely, and he began to relate the details of some of the activities of which he was suspicious. I said that I could appreciate how concerned he was about these situations but that there were other people waiting to be seen, and I thought it would be better if he would tell his story to someone who could take some action regarding it. Reluctantly he agreed to take his complaints elsewhere.

I then asked him how much he understood about an auxiliary police patrolman's job. He proceeded to list the various responsibilities, which indicated that he had read pretty carefully the descriptive pamphlet given to him with the application form. I was interested that he stated each of these responsibilities in a punitive manner: "Keep the kids from hanging around and tossing cigarette butts and gum papers on the sidewalk." "Make the people clean up their yards." "Stop people from burning leaves." And so on.

Then he added with a gleam in his eye, "You know, most Americans need a strong arm to get them to do things." I asked him what he would do if he came across a man who refused to obey orders. Without a moment's hesitation he responded that if the man was his size, he thought he would "sock him" and get some other men to take him away; if the man was bigger than he, he would call the police.

I asked him what qualifications he thought he had for this position, and he replied that he was in good health, he was not a "drinking man," and he was "always on time," never late for work in his life. I commented that these were important qualifications, and I wondered whether they might not be more useful in some other line of work than the one he had chosen. I said the Community Action Program wanted to know about each person's special abilities and skills so that the person might be placed in the particular job in which these qualifications might be used to greatest advantage. Mr. Robertson eagerly asked whether I thought there was a better kind of job for him, and then I suggested that he specify his second and third choices on the basis of what his work experience had best trained him to do.

Mr. Robertson then told me about his clerical experience and revealed that he was apparently exceptionally precise and accurate with figures. I encouraged him to talk more about his work experiences. I learned that he would get along at a job quite well for several months but then would become bored with the monotony and also critical of authority. In each instance the criticism seemed to develop to the point of his feeling justified in quitting, and thus it was the course he would take.

I stressed the advantages of this office training and pointed out that there would be far fewer persons with his qualifications than with those necessary for auxiliary police patrol. I then asked him, "If the Program should ask you to take an assignment that involved your skills with figures, would you accept it?" Magnanimously he agreed to take such a job but then asked quickly, "Would I be given a badge to wear for that kind of work?"

I asked him why he inquired. Rather sheepishly, he protested that he did not know. He had just seen some group pictures of volunteer auxiliary police in another community with badges of office, and it gave them a look of importance and authority that had impressed him. I said I guessed that wanting to look important was pretty natural after all. I was not sure whether he would be given a badge, but he could be sure that, no matter what assignment he was given, it would be given on the basis that the Community Action Program felt it needed him in that particular spot. He said that certainly was enough for him, thanked me, and left.

The outstanding skill illustrated in this interview is the worker's ability to guide this man's planning into more constructive channels without in any way threatening him, punishing him for his punitive attitudes, or pointing out to him his unfitness for the auxiliary police patrol job. She refrains from any attempt to change his personality but rather redirects his energies so that he might be able to use them helpfully instead of harmfully. Through her skilled questioning she first hears about some of his attitudes that would make him unsuited for the job (but she does not tell him everything she has observed or thought). Then she proceeds by further questioning to discover what abilities he does have and to assure him that they are needed fully as much as are the services of the auxiliary police patrol. Thus, he is able to shift his plans without any loss of his personal dignity, and at the same time the neighborhood is saved from what otherwise promises to be some unfortunate brawls.

At the end, one of his probable subjective reasons for wanting to be an auxiliary police patrolman is revealed in his question about the badge. We get a glimpse here, beneath the surface of a self-assured, arrogant man, of a little boy impressed with uniforms and badges.

This interview presents a slightly different situation, since the applicant is not seeking help in the sense of going to a social agency. There are many interviews in which the situation is similar. The interviewer does not have the responsibility of helping the individual with his problems but rather of determining his potentiality for meeting certain requirements. Typical interviews that come to mind in this connection are those with prospective foster parents or adoptive parents. They come to the agency not to seek help for themselves but to offer their services. It is the responsibility of the interviewer, however, to determine enough about their personalities and capacities to evaluate their ability to do the job for which they are volunteering. In these instances the interviewer's primary responsibility is to protect his client, for example, the child needing a home; but in doing so he often has an opportunity to be indirectly helpful to the person who has applied.

12

"You Want Me to Go Home Today?"

The following interview from a rehabilitation agency illustrates how the use of supportive, nonjudgmental comments enables a handicapped woman to decide to return to her work after an outburst of anger directed at her supervisor in the workshop.

When I arrived at the workshop late Friday morning, I was greeted by the nurse, who informed me that Mrs. Green had been sent out of the work area and was on her way to the social service department. The nurse reminded me that during her six months in the workshop Mrs. Green had tended to be domineering and had frequently had outbursts of anger. I barely had time to look at Mrs. Green's record and learn that she had many physical problems, including cerebral palsy and related cerebral dysfunction, and that she was of low average intelligence, when Mrs. Green arrived. She was an attractive-looking, middle-aged woman with an unsteady walk and severe head and body tremors. I introduced myself, and she responded with a tremulous smile and an air of false bravado, saying: "Hello. You want me to go home today?"

I suggested that we go into my office to talk. En route she kept mumbling, "What kind of man is he? Is he a person?"

After we were seated, Mrs. Green tried unsuccessfully to hold back her tears as she went on a verbal tirade about her supervisor, Pete. "He's so cruel, like an animal. He gives me all the work no one else wants to do. Where did he come from? Is this a place to work or a popularity contest?" I asked what she meant, and she stated that Pete had his favorite "chicks." She added, "I am not going to fold those sheets and stand on my feet all day." I said I could understand if there were some tasks she could not do and asked whether the problem was that she could not fold the plastic sheets. Mrs. Green reacted in a furious way and retorted: "Of course I can do the work, but I want to sit down. I won't go back there; I'll go home." I replied that going home for the day might be a temporary solution—and the best one for now— but first, I would like to telephone the workshop manager about the possibility that Mrs. Green could sit while she worked.

As I reached for the phone, Mrs. Green became quiet and looked like a guilty child. She said, "I better tell you I insulted Pete." I postponed the call and asked about the "insults." Mrs. Green repeated several derogatory remarks she had made, including "Drop dead!" I said she must have felt pretty unhappy and upset to have made these remarks. Could she tell me why she was so upset? Mrs. Green started to

"You Want Me to Go Home Today?"
135

berate Pete, saying, "All the girls like him, and of course he likes them best because they're all healthy, not like where I worked before." I asked what it was like where she worked before, and Mrs. Green explained that for ten years she had attended a workshop for the physically handicapped but that here she was one of only a few workers who were handicapped. (I realized that she did not consider or understand that the workshop clients with psychiatric diagnoses were "handicapped.") I explained that the other workers in the shop who looked so "healthy" to Mrs. Green still had problems and needed the workshop just as much as she did. I said I hoped she could consider returning to work that day, but before she did we had better discuss her behavior. We would like to help her find a way to remain in the program, but she could not stay if she continued to insult people.

Mrs. Green referred to Pete: "Is he some important person? Maybe he's a spy. They told me he goes abroad lots of times." I said, firmly, that Pete was not a spy and added that he was an important person in the workshop and so was she. Mrs. Green looked surprised, then pleased, then questioning. "You mean me—'Shaky Annie'?" I said maybe one of the problems in regard to the workshop might be her feeling that neither Pete nor the other workers liked her, and she wanted to be liked just as everyone does. Mrs. Green replied: "That's true, but I can't help how I am. I've always been like this and I always will be. I was always in the slow classes in school. I know I can't walk right, and I shake more when I get upset—like today." I said she had accomplished a great deal because she had been in the other workshop program for so many years. When I asked about her life away from work, I learned that Mr. Green also had cerebral palsy, was judged legally blind, and attended a workshop for the blind. They maintained their own apartment, and Mrs. Green did the cooking, cleaning, and shopping.

I emphasized Mrs. Green's ability by enumerating all the things she could do and supported her decision to return to work that day rather than go home. I then telephoned the workshop manager, who agreed that Mrs. Green could sit at work whenever she wished to do so.

I suggested to Mrs. Green that a neurological reevaluation might be helpful. If a reassessment of her medication indicated a change in the prescription, it could lead to better control of the tremors and outbursts of anger. By this time Mrs. Green was calm and was ready to return to work. She smiled and offered a promise "to behave." When she asked if I would see her later in the day, I assured her I would be available if she needed me but that I would not schedule an appointment for an interview. Mrs. Green returned to the workshop.

The worker knows that Mrs. Green's behavior in the workshop has been troublesome on many previous occasions, but she does not make any reference to this fact in the early part of the interview. It is only later, after Mrs. Green has admitted that she had insulted the supervisor, that the worker refers to behavior that needs to be changed.

When Mrs. Green's response to the worker's greeting shows an attempt to conceal anxiety with bravado, the worker invites her into the office, where they can talk in privacy. The worker does not respond to Mrs. Green's question—an offer to return home, instead of being "sent" home, that reveals her insecurity and expectation of punishment. Her comments about the supervisor and the harsh accusations against him, which the worker knows cannot be true, give the first clue to a possible cause of Mrs. Green's upset state. The worker does not, however, challenge Mrs. Green's statements nor does she defend the supervisor. The worker listens and notes that Mrs. Green views herself as the rejected worker ("He gives me all the work no one else wants to do") and views the other women as the favored workers (Mrs. Green loses out in the "popularity contest").

When Mrs. Green announces she will not do a specific task, the worker apparently assumes she cannot physically do it, a notion that elicits an angry denial from Mrs. Green. The worker's comment, about an inability to perform some tasks, stems from her concern about a handicapped person. Mrs. Green's reactions show that she resents any insinuation that she is incapable of doing her job, but she wants some allowance made for her condition. Had the worker been more sensitive to the possible implication of inadequacy in her question, she would have made a different comment, perhaps an inquiry as to why Mrs. Green disliked folding the plastic cloths, for example. However, the worker's question does not prove to be wholly unfortunate, because the client's response reveals that work is important to her and that she wants her individual needs recognized.

Knowing how important work is to Mrs. Green, the worker realizes it would be a great blow to her self-esteem to be "sent" home. Instead, the worker helps Mrs. Green to demonstrate her ability to work: she offers to intervene in the work assignment, to find out whether Mrs. Green can be permitted to sit rather than stand.

Responding to the worker's obvious interest in and concern for her, Mrs. Green, like a child, "confesses" her misdeed: she insulted the supervisor. The worker's matter-of-fact acceptance of her behavior and the worker's expressed understanding that unhappiness must have provoked such behavior are crucial in enabling Mrs. Green to reveal her feelings of inadequacy and difference because of her handicaps. In her previous work setting, where everyone else had obvious physical handicaps, Mrs. Green did not feel so different and, perhaps, was less vulnerable to feelings that she was being discriminated against or slighted in any way. The worker's perception that Mrs. Green recognizes only physical conditions as handicapping leads to her simple explanation that the other persons have the same need for the workshop as Mrs. Green has. The worker then directs Mrs. Green's attention to considering whether she can return to the workshop. Wisely, the worker keeps her interpretation of the other persons brief and simple. Mrs. Green needs consideration for herself, and she would not be receptive to a discussion of the needs or problems of her co-workers.

When the worker suggests discussing Mrs. Green's behavior in the workshop and the need to control it, Mrs. Green refers again to Pete. As if to bolster her case against him, she brings up the possibility that he might be a spy. The worker appropriately does not encourage this thinking but states firmly that it is not true. The worker asserts that Pete is an important person in the workshop and adds a comment that has great meaning to Mrs. Green: ". . . and so are you." Mrs. Green reacts first with an expression of surprise, then pleasure, then a questioning look because it has always seemed clear to her that, with her peculiar walk and uncontrolled body movements, she could not be an "important" person. When she is referred to as "important," she reveals her feelings of inadequacy and the fact that in school she was always placed in the slow classes.

Mrs. Green refers to her handicaps after the worker has affirmed how normal it is for Mrs. Green to want to be liked by her supervisor and co-workers. Mrs. Green's image of herself, especially her feeling that she is not liked, is so negative that she seems hopeless about herself. Furthermore, she realizes that when she becomes upset her physical symptoms increase. It may be tempting, when faced with such an unhappy and handicapped person, to express sympathy or exhort the person to "cheer up." Such a response, however, could result in strengthening a feeling of hopelessness—one's situation is truly so bad the worker can only agree with its futility. The worker does not succumb to this natural inclination. Instead, she reminds Mrs. Green of her long work record and asks about her life when she is not at work. Mrs. Green's attention is thus directed to her strengths rather than her handicaps, and she recounts the many daily tasks she and her handicapped husband successfully perform. The worker can validly attest to Mrs. Green's competence in many areas of daily living, and when Mrs. Green decides to return to her job, the worker, knowing more now of this woman's ability to surmount difficulties, can encourage her to do so.

The telephone call to the workshop manager is an instance of help with a specific complaint that Mrs. Green has made. It is accepted as a reasonable one, and meeting this need is evidence of the worker's interest in Mrs. Green. The worker's concern is further demonstrated by the suggestion, based on her knowledge of similar situations, that the medication for Mrs. Green be reviewed by the neurologist. Hope is held out to Mrs. Green that she may have further medical help in controlling her behavior and physical condition. Like a child, Mrs. Green gives the worker a promise of good behavior and tentatively asks about seeing the worker later in the day. The worker agrees to be available if Mrs. Green needs to talk further with her but indicates her expectation that she can manage on her own. With this response, the worker again keeps a realistic focus on the strengths evidenced by her client and helps a severely handicapped woman maintain her ability to cope with emotional and physical stress.

13

"What's Going to Happen to Me Now?"

The following two interviews from a child welfare agency show how interviewing may be used in preparing a child for placement. By means of her friendly interest and considerate explanations, the worker is able to change the child's hopeless anxiety in the face of a new and frightening situation into an acceptance of the change and even a certain expectancy that it will mean better days ahead. The child is freed from the feeling of being "pushed around" by having an opportunity to participate in preparations for the change.

[Elaine, aged eleven, was referred to the intake division of a child welfare agency by the children's court for placement away from home. The court report stated that for about a year Elaine's stepfather had been engaged in sexual activities with her. Elaine, who had been born out of wedlock, had already gone through a series of unhealthy experiences because of her mother's promiscuity.

The court had given Elaine physical, psychological, and psychiatric examinations and had found her healthy, intelligent, and friendly, but very much upset about her experiences with her stepfather. She had been afraid to confide in her mother because her stepfather had threatened to kill her if she did. The psychiatrist recommended that Elaine be placed away from home, at least until her mother proved able to maintain a stable home.

In considering the type of care that would best meet Elaine's needs, the agency decided that a cottage-plan institution might be preferable at this time to a foster home. It was thought that it might be easier for her to adjust first in an institution where she would have an opportunity to relate herself to children and would have a wider choice in selecting an adult with whom she could identify. In planning Elaine's first placement in an institution, the agency hoped that after she had had an opportunity to readjust her first concepts of an adult world, she might then be placed in a foster home.

At the time of the court's referral to the agency, she had already spent three months at a children's detention home while the court's investigation was being made. Her mother had opposed placement but was finally forced to accept the authority of the court. Because of the delay in referral, the worker had only two days in which to prepare Elaine for placement. The following are her accounts of her two interviews with Elaine.]

I first visited Elaine at the children's detention home. Before seeing Elaine, I arranged to take her out for an hour the following afternoon. I saw Elaine for about forty-five minutes.

She was totally unprepared for my visit. She was completely bewildered by her present experience and asked, "What's going to happen to me now?" Elaine, a small, olive-skinned girl, thin and pathetic, with straight brown hair and a heart-shaped face, appeared quite terrified when she was brought down and introduced to me. She had tried unsuccessfully to improve her appearance by combing her hair in the latest fashion. The faded, ill-fitting clothes provided by the detention home did not improve her appearance. Her very large, dark eyes were sad, and several times tears welled up in her eyes and flowed down her cheeks. At times she seemed unable to speak because she would cry. In the midst of her tears she attempted to smile. Her lips would quiver. She would try to control herself, be unable to, cry, and then look up from under her lashes and try to brave a smile.

I introduced myself to Elaine, explaining that the court had asked our help in planning for her. I said I knew that she was unhappy in the detention home and bewildered about what was going to happen to her. Insofar as I could, in the short time we had, I would like to help her. Elaine's face lit up, and she tried very hard to smile, to show her appreciation, but it was difficult for her to smile without tears. Elaine and I spent some time discussing her present experience in the detention home. She told me that she had lost a good deal of weight since she had been there, both because she was unhappy and because she could not eat the food they served. She continued to talk about the detention home, expressing a great deal of resentment.

With a sad expression she said that she had been there longer than most of the children, and she thought it was a very long time. The monotony was relieved a little by visits from relatives. On the morning of the day I was there her mother, her sister, and her aunt had come to see her. With real feeling the child said, "My mother wants to take me home." She cried in a heartbreaking fashion. I said I was sure that her mother wanted to take her home but that perhaps it was not possible for her to go home yet. Her mother would first make a real home for her, and then she would go to live with her mother. Elaine continued to cry and to say that she wanted to go home with her mother, that she did not want to go anywhere else. With a sigh, the child said that she knew she really could not go home yet. The judge had talked to her, and he had explained to her that it was best for her to live somewhere else. In front of the judge her mother had said that she would try to make a good home for Elaine. Elaine said she had accepted the fact that she was going to be sent someplace. She was sure her mother would do everything to make it possible to take her home in the very near future; until that time, however, some other plan had to be made for her. She did not know what that plan was, but she felt sure that I could tell her.

Did my visit mean that I could get her out of the detention home? I said that was what I wanted to do and was why I had come to see her, to talk to her about what was going to happen to her. Elaine said that strange things had been happening to her. Until the past few months she had not known about courts and judges and "horrible places" like the detention home. I said that these were unusual experiences for a child and painful ones. Elaine cried bitterly. She was so eager to get out of the home. She had not even been out of the building for the past three months. I said I had made arrangements to take her out for a walk the following day. We would spend an hour together, and she could plan the hour in whatever way she liked. At this point Elaine gave me a really genuine smile, and I commented on it, saying that I had not been sure she knew how to smile; that when she smiled her face lit up, she was so pretty. Elaine managed a laugh at that and said she would spend the rest of her waking hours planning for our time the next day. I said that besides taking her out, I wanted to talk with her about some other matters.

Her change in residence would come about in two days. I thought she might like to know something about the place to which she was going. Elaine shyly smiled and said that she would. I told her about the physical setup; the name, which she thought was very nice; the sewing class; the school; the activities in the institution; and so on. Elaine said that she could crochet and that she was making a washcloth. She was interested in the sewing class. She was also interested in the toys. Elaine said she could ride a bicycle and could skate. She liked to cook, and the idea of helping in the cottages appealed to her. She told me some of the things she could cook and was pleased that she could make rather fancy dishes. She was interested in the library at the institution and said that she had previously belonged to a library. She asked about the ages of the children there, about the cottage mothers, and so on.

I said that the whole idea of this institution must be very new to Elaine. Since I was sure she could not at that time think of all the questions she would like to ask, I would leave her a pencil and paper, and she could write down all the questions that came to her mind. When I saw her the following day, we could go over the list of questions. Elaine seemed very pleased with this arrangement—more pleased, I thought, because she was keeping something tangible to remind her that I was real than because she would be able to ask questions. (This thought was confirmed the next day. Although Elaine had left the paper and pencil upstairs, she remembered all the questions she wanted to ask me.) Elaine squeezed my hand when I left her and became very cheerful when she said she would be dressed and ready to go out for a walk when I came the following day.

The following day I met Elaine at the detention home. She was dressed in her own clothes and ready to go out. When I first came, she was smiling broadly and ran to meet me. Although her clothes were torn and patched, her appearance was dignified. She took my hand immediately and held it tightly throughout the hour we spent together.

Elaine had planned the hour in this way: She first wanted to walk in the sunshine; then she wanted to go to a department store and look at the toys. It was interesting to watch Elaine change from a dignified, stiff little girl into a prancing, happy child. She fairly danced after she got used to me and the freedom and the fresh air. When she was ready, we went to the department store she selected and immediately took the elevator up to the toy department. When we had entered the store, Elaine had looked at me coyly and said that she would like to start with the boys' side first. She was interested in most of the boys' toys, particularly in an electric train. With a cute smile and a flirtatious glance she said, "In my neighborhood I'm known as quite a tomboy." When we finished the boys' side and went to the girls' side, Elaine was much less interested. Occasionally she would comment on a doll, saying that she had one like it or her sister had one like it. On the whole, she was not interested in the girls' toys. On the way out of the store we stopped at a fountain to get a drink. Elaine had a pineapple soda with chocolate ice cream, which she drank with a good deal of gusto, getting every last drop out of the glass.

During the hour we were able to talk a little about the institution. Occasionally she would see a toy and ask whether they had one like it there. Elaine was also able to get from me the details of what would be happening to her the following day in court. I explained that I would not be there because I had to be at the institution on that day. Since I would be at the institution, I would, however, have an opportunity to tell them about her so that they would be expecting her when she came. I gave her a brief description of the people she would meet when she first got there.

When we got back to the detention home, Elaine said that the hour had passed all too fast. When I got ready to leave, she thanked me and looked up at me with a sort of questioning look. I leaned over and the child put both arms around my neck and kissed me. She then turned her face away and giggled. I gave her a reassuring smile and squeezed her hand; then she went upstairs with the matron.

Elaine comes to life for us in the interviewer's vivid portrayal. The description reveals a discerning observation of a child. In all adequate interviewing, even as the external greetings are taking place, internal mental notes are being made. The worker's first activity is always guided by his early observations. Here the worker immediately sees a frightened, bewildered child. As a result, she takes the initiative, for she realizes that a child precipitated into such a bewildering situation would feel lost, anxious, and insecure in the face of an unknown future. Having been plunged into an unfamiliar detention home, not knowing from day to day what may happen to her, Elaine feels completely at the mercy of grown-ups. She is filled with a sense of futility and helplessness in the face of their overpowering strength and authority.

In addition to realizing how the girl feels, the caseworker knows that she must take the initiative because Elaine has not asked for an interview and has no idea why she is being sought out. The worker, therefore, attempts to put the child at ease by telling her at once why she has come, thus freeing her as much as possible from her natural fear of another new and perhaps calamitous experience. The worker indicates that she wants to be Elaine's friend, something a child can understand. She lets Elaine know also that she understands how Elaine feels about the detention home, as well as her feelings of uncertainty about what will happen to her.

One important aspect of the first interview consists in allowing the child to express—what she had been unable to mention with others—her dislike of the detention home and her unhappiness there. Another is the worker's attempt to visualize as simply and concretely as possible for Elaine what she can expect in the new home to which she will be going. As concrete evidence to the child of her friendliness, she arranges to take her out of the home for an hour and promises to let Elaine choose how they will spend that time. If Elaine had not been given any opportunity to talk against the detention home, she might have had to bottle up her resentment. By expressing herself, she "gets it off her chest." Further, the very fact of the worker's sympathetic understanding makes it possible for Elaine to regard her many recent troubles as less intolerably unjust.

Although the worker takes the initiative in this interview, it is initiative of a quite different sort from that taken by the court in placing the child in the detention home with a vague explanation. The initiative of the worker stimulates Elaine to participate in the plans being made. It is valuable for even a young child to have some feeling that he has a share in important decisions about his own future. It may not be possible to allow Elaine to choose, for instance, whether she will remain with her mother or live away from home, whether she will live in an institution or a foster home, or to choose the institution or foster home in which she will live. In these areas the agency must take the responsibility for her protection and use its better judgment. Elaine would have no basis on which to make such choices. We cannot make a free choice unless we know what the alternatives are. In the face of these necessary limitations, the worker arranges for an hour's walk during which Elaine will be completely free to determine what they will do. An ingenious worker will always find some areas in which she can leave decisions to her client, stimulating him to initiative and independent choice and giving him the feeling that he still has some control of the situation.

Here, the worker also does what she can to let Elaine participate as much as possible in the plans being made for her. She is encouraged to talk about them whenever she has enough interest and knowledge to do so. For instance, the worker offers to answer any questions about the new home that come to Elaine's mind, but she does not volunteer information beyond Elaine's present interest or ken.

Elaine might have asked, "Will they want a little girl like me who has been bad?" In that case the worker might have talked with her further about her experiences with her stepfather, but because Elaine did not bring these experiences up, the worker did not push her. Undoubtedly Elaine will need to talk with someone about the experiences she has had, but if the worker had at such an early point indicated that she wanted Elaine to talk about them, Elaine might well have felt that it was too soon to discuss such matters with a stranger.

The worker implies by her attitude that she understands and wants to help, and that there will be others in the new home who will help. Her acceptance of the child's resentment against the detention home gives Elaine some security by showing her that there are understanding people in the world with whom one can talk. The worker's sensitive observation of the child's slightest expression is indicated in her recognition of Elaine's desire to kiss her. The worker's natural, unembarrassed response is an appropriate one to a frightened, friendless child.

The concrete purpose of these interviews was to prepare Elaine to be emotionally ready to accept a new home so that she could go into it with some feeling of security. Such preparation was especially important here because Elaine's many unfortunate experiences would otherwise have led her to expect the worst from another sudden change thrust upon her. This attitude would, in turn, have jeopardized the success of her placement. The danger was lessened by the interviewer's leading Elaine to look forward with hope to going to her new home.

14

"You Better Not Laugh at Me"

The following interview with a confused, rebellious college student illustrates how skillful interviewing can be used effectively in meeting an emergency and in initiating steps to provide continuing professional help to improve the family situation that caused the emergency.

Richard Randall walked briskly up to the Travelers Aid Society desk in the railroad station. He was smiling, but in an anxious voice blurted out that he was in desperate need of help and "You better not laugh at me." I asked why he thought I would regard his situation as funny, although he himself was smiling.

Richard, age eighteen, was a tall, slim, nice-looking fellow dressed in blue jeans, a sweat shirt, and a presentable jacket. Somewhat defiantly he announced that the previous morning he had left his college (about two hundred miles from this city), had sold his books, and was hitchhiking to New York. I commented that he was taking this action just before the spring vacation and asked what he was planning to do. He said that he expected to live a Bohemian life in Greenwich Village and become a writer. Before I could respond, he hastily stated that I must be wondering what "a nice boy with a good background" was doing hitchhiking in this fashion. He added that these plans were not what he wanted to talk about; they were not his immediate concern, for nothing I could say would dissuade him from going to New York. He had come to TAS, at the suggestion of a suburban policeman, for help in retrieving his stolen luggage and money. Because his urgent focus was on this subject, I decided it was best to so gear our discussion, in the hope that he might later be able to tackle the problems that had precipitated his present plight. I asked what had happened to his luggage and money.

Richard explained that he had left school with about ten dollars in cash, intending to hitchhike to New York. It had taken him all day to get as far as the outskirts of this city. The weather was bad—there had been a heavy snowfall, and it was extremely cold—and he had spent the night at an all-night restaurant.

He had sat up talking with various people, particularly another young fellow whom he knew only as Jerry. He thought Jerry was a local boy who spent much time "just hanging around that place." He had told Jerry much of his situation and what he was trying to do, and early that morning Jerry had sympathetically offered to help him get a reduced-fare bus ticket to New York through the company for which he worked. He had driven Richard part way into town and had left him in a suburban restaurant. After Richard had given him six dollars toward the cost of the ticket, Jerry had driven off with Richard's luggage in the car; he had said he would be back in ten minutes. Richard had waited an hour and then had finally come to the realization that he had been "taken." He had been furious with himself for his own naiveté. Determined to do something about the theft, he had gone to the police, who had suggested that he either return to where he and Jerry had met and appeal to the state police there or apply to the Travelers Aid Society. He had decided to follow the second suggestion.

Richard had been sufficiently observant of his companion to be able to give an accurate physical description of Jerry and his car, as well as some bits of information about others who might know him. When I helped Richard communicate with the state police, they were interested and were willing to pursue the matter. In fact, because Richard could not easily return to their area, they offered to send one of their officers to our office to talk with him.

When I asked where he wanted to wait for the officer, Richard said, "In your office, if it's okay with you." I said it was, and noticing that he seemed to be more relaxed, I casually referred to his earlier comment about his "good background." Richard responded that he was feeling more inclined to talk about himself now. He expressed strongly rebellious feelings against his parents and said, "I've been in this state for at least the past year." I asked what seemed to be the trouble between him and his parents. Using descriptive vocabulary, he spoke of his parents' "mediocrity," their "upper-middle-class materialistic values," their "lack of understanding," the fact that he and they simply did not operate on the same level and that he was "sick and tired of eating their money and studying their money." So he had decided to do something about it. Impulsively, he had decided to go to New York and had sold his books. He had asked his roommate to forward the weekly check from his father to him in New York. He had told his parents nothing about his plan.

He said he thought his special skills might lie in writing; although he had been a fairly good student, he had no interest in any other field. I asked him whether he could tell me more about his plans. He replied by expressing considerable confusion about what he was doing, what he wanted to do, and how to go about achieving any goals he might decide upon. He spoke disdainfully of what he viewed as his mother's naiveté, her prudishness in regard to sex, and her resistance to ever discussing the subject with him. Obviously he was testing me as he spoke with deliberate brashness about his views, but I voiced no judgment on his opinions. Because I thought he was expecting me to lecture him as his parents probably had done, I carefully tried to refrain from making any judgmental statements about his actions. I did, however, question him about what he hoped to accomplish by this impulsive move and departure from school. I suggested that we think about the realities of how he actually would manage and what such a change of plans might mean eventually to himself and to his parents. Despite his earlier rebellious expressions about his parents, he was willing to concede that his folks were "decent enough" people, but he was not interested in their way of life. He felt particularly strongly about never being able to achieve any kind of understanding relationship with his mother. He stated that his father "wasn't a bad sort of guy" and that he could at least talk a bit with him. He commented that in fact his father probably did know more about life than Richard, for he would have never permitted himself to be conned as Richard had been.

He became silent and seemed to be engrossed in

thought. I made no comment, and in a few seconds he said he thought perhaps he was an object of concern and irritation to his parents, who had adopted him when he was two months old. When I asked why he thought he had this effect on them, he said it was because of something that had happened last summer. I asked whether it was something he could tell me about, and he responded that "it might be a good idea to let you know" that the tension at home had come to a serious point last summer following his attempt at suicide with an overdose of tranquilizers. After this episode Richard had had some psychiatric treatment, but he could not indicate whether it had been helpful to him. He knew his parents worried a great deal about him and wanted him to continue treatment. His attitude toward their concern led me to wonder whether he had used treatment as a kind of threat or manipulative device against his parents; I did not, however, comment on this thought. I asked if he thought that professional counseling might help him think through what he wanted as goals for himself. He replied crisply, "That might be a good idea."

Richard then began to insist that he was going on to New York regardless of anything else. He did not make this statement with conviction, and I had the feeling he was trying to convince himself rather than me that this plan was advisable. I suggested we ought to think about some of the possible difficulties he might still encounter. As we reviewed what had happened so far on his trip, he indicated more uncertainty about the advisability of continuing. In a doubtful tone he finally asked me whether he should go ahead with his plan. I replied: "Maybe you would like to think about returning to school instead. What would be involved in this kind of plan?" Richard began to point out some minor obstacles but then said he really wanted to go back to school.

He would like to retrieve his belongings, get on a bus, return to school, and forget that this hitchhiking episode had ever occurred. He added that his parents need never know about it. I said I thought it probably was what he really wanted to do—to return to school—and I would be glad to help him with such a plan, but I did not think that the situation could be handled quite in the fashion he suggested. I said that from all he had told me there did seem to be a serious breakdown in his relationship with his parents and that, unless some effort was made by Richard and his parents to achieve some better understanding, the feelings that led to his leaving school could perhaps produce additional problems. I also said that even though Richard was a young man of eighteen, I felt I had an obligation to advise his parents of his whereabouts and his current situation, because actually he did need both their emotional and financial help at the moment. With some reluctance Richard agreed to my notifying his parents.

Richard then volunteered that he knew he needed professional help, and he decried the fact that nothing but academic counseling seemed to exist at his college. He said he did get concerned because he had so many decisions to make about college and then about what he finally wanted to do. I explained to Richard that I would communicate with the Travelers Aid Society in his home city, whose worker would arrange to talk to his parents and discuss the plans for his return to school the next day. I also told him that the worker would be glad to talk with all of them about the possibility of ongoing help for Richard and perhaps for his parents. I assured him that the worker there would follow through on helping him get the counseling that he needed. Richard liked this suggestion. He said it was only a short time until spring vacation. He was certain he could manage all right until then. And if his parents talked to the Travelers Aid worker before he got home, he and they might be better able to discuss how they could improve their communication as well as how much help his parents could give him in returning to professional treatment. Richard then asked if he could make a collect call to his school roommate about holding the check for him. It turned out to be a wise move because the roommate was just on his way to mail Richard's check to him in New York. Richard did not go into detail but merely advised his friend that he had much to tell him. The important point was that he was giving up his plans to continue on to New York, and he would be returning to school.

When the police reported they had located Jerry and needed Richard to identify him the next day, I arranged for Richard's food and lodging for the night. The following day, after recovering his luggage, Richard returned to the office. I told him that his parents had talked with the TAS worker in their city, had deposited money for his return fare to school, and had expressed willingness to help Richard obtain counseling. Richard looked pleased and relieved when I added that his parents were looking forward to seeing him during the spring vacation and wanted to try to improve their relationship.

The worker's first observation is the contrast between the young man's approach—his attempt to create the impression of a self-confident, untroubled person—and his anxious voice. Similarly, although he is smiling, he is fearful of being ridiculed. The worker, noting these inconsistencies, correctly surmises that his manner is only a superficial veneer and that he is trying very hard to conceal a feeling of fright. His expectation of being laughed at alerts the worker to the possibility that his "desperate need" of help may be caused by actions he considers childish or foolish on his part. Her response assures him she will take his situation seriously despite his initial approach.

Still anticipating criticism, Richard fends off any discussion of his plans or his family background and makes it clear he wants help only with a practical problem: retrieving his luggage and money. The worker, therefore, focuses on his request for help with a specific, obvious problem. Her questions are intended to elicit the facts about his loss of luggage and money and to enable Richard to tell the story of his experience with Jerry. The revelation of his lack of sophistication explains his fear of being laughed at. He is angry at himself and expects to be criticized for his naiveté. The worker does not comment on what happened but matter of factly helps Richard get in touch with the state police. His relief after taking this step is so obvious that the worker assumes, correctly, that he may now be more willing to talk about his family situation. Also, his wish to remain in her office may indicate a desire to talk further with her.

Having found the worker noncritical and helpful in the area he has specified as the one in which he wants help, Richard becomes less defensive and is able to reveal the long-standing problems in his relationship to his parents, especially his mother. His impulsive decision to leave college and embark on a vague plan to become a writer appears to be a running away from an increasingly stressful situation. As the worker, carefully noncommittal, shows interest in his plans, he reveals even more confusion and lack of clarity in planning and goals for himself. He tries to shock the worker by telling her his views on sex. Again the worker avoids the pitfall of responding to his provocation and reacting as a parent might. Her focus on the realities of his situation and the possible results for his future enables Richard to begin to think more realistically.

After a brief silence, which the worker respects, Richard reveals the extent of the friction with his parents and his attempted suicide of the previous summer followed by a period of psychiatric treatment. Recognizing the seriousness of his upset and the extent of his present confusion and rebellion, the worker focuses on the value of his getting professional counsel. Although Richard readily agrees, he makes one last, feeble attempt to continue with his act of rebellion. Rather than argue the wisdom of this plan, the worker suggests they consider possible difficulties. When he finally asks the worker's advice, she, understanding his ambivalence, suggests he *might* like to think about returning to school. When this plan proves to be what he really wants, he suggests a course of action that he hopes will enable him to forget that this episode ever happened. The worker, however, does not encourage such thinking. She knows it could be another running away from his problems. She reminds him, gently, of the troubled relationships in his family and the reality of his present need for emotional and financial help from his parents. Richard's acceptance of her interest in him and his welfare leads him to agree, reluctantly, to notifying his parents of his situation. He then expresses his concern about how to obtain counseling help, and the worker immediately assures him of the availability to him and his parents of the services of a TAS worker in his home community.

The worker's ability to refrain from judgmental comments stemmed from her perception that Richard's behavior (despite his confusion and impulsive actions) was an attempt to assert himself as an independent person, albeit a confused and deeply troubled one. By concentrating first on the practical aspects of his predicament, the worker demonstrated her interest in helping Richard. Perhaps sensing that the worker was not reacting like a "typical" adult, Richard could begin to talk about himself and reveal his need for further help.

The worker then learned the extent of Richard's upset emotional state, when he told of an attempt at suicide and a brief period of psychiatric help during the previous summer. Aware of his present confusion and indecision, and to prevent his again "running away" psychologically, the worker took responsibility for involving his parents. Richard was not enthusiastic about this suggestion, but the worker's simple explanation that in reality he needed his parents at this time was accepted by him. Thus, a perceptive worker, through sensitive, nonthreatening interviewing, was able to lay the groundwork for the more extensive help that Richard and his parents sorely needed.

15

"I Will Not Go Back"

The interview that follows illustrates a medical social worker's sensitivity in recognizing the feelings of loss and loneliness that underlie an elderly woman's stubborn refusal to return to a nursing home. It also illustrates the importance of gently helping a client to accept a reality that cannot be altered and of doing it in such a way that her sense of self-worth is left intact.

[Mrs. Benson, seventy-nine years of age, was brought to the attention of the hospital social service department by a resident physician. It was late afternoon on the day before Thanksgiving. Mrs. Benson had come to the hospital by taxi from the western part of the state, expecting to be admitted for treatment. In the judgment of the examining physicians,

Mrs. Benson did not need hospital care. She refused, however, to leave the hospital and could not be persuaded to do so, either by the doctors or the nurses. The resident physician suggested that an interview with the social worker might be helpful to Mrs. Benson in accepting the fact that she could not be admitted. The caseworker's interview follows.]

I found Mrs. Benson sitting in a wheelchair, surrounded by a doctor and several nurses, her suitcase by her side. When I was introduced, she glowered and said, "I will not go back." When I asked her where she lived, she named a nursing home in her town. Still glaring angrily, she asserted: "You can't make me go back. I want to be in the hospital. I'm sick." I said I knew that she had come to the hospital expecting to be admitted but that the doctors thought she was well enough to go home. She said, "I know how I feel better than the doctors do, and I am sick." I said I realized it was difficult to understand, but the doctors could not let a person stay in the hospital unless they thought it necessary. Mrs. Benson looked at me long and hard but said nothing.

I tried to engage Mrs. Benson in conversation by asking her some simple questions, but she maintained a total silence, lowered her head, and looked sad and angry. I realized that it must be a bit overwhelming for her to be surrounded by several people who were staring at her and who were as determined as she was. I asked, "Would you mind if I wheeled you over to those chairs so I can sit down with you for a bit?" She shook her head but said nothing. I pushed her chair to a corner of the room and sat down beside her. The doctor and the nurses drifted away.

I commented: "You look weary. Have you had a long day here today?" She nodded, and after a pause she said, "I've been here since nine o'clock this morning." (It was then almost 5:00 P.M.) I said, "Oh dear, I bet you had to wait a very long time to see the doctor." She nodded and said that because she had come without an appointment, it had been a long wait before the doctor had examined her. I asked her if she had had any lunch. She said that she had not; she had had breakfast before she had left the nursing home. I said: "You must be hungry. Would you like me to get you a sandwich and some milk or coffee?" She replied, "I would just like to go to the bathroom, but I can't get there by myself." I said: "Why don't I ask the nurse to take you to the bathroom, and I'll go downstairs to see what kind of sandwiches there are in the machine. When you get back you can tell me what might taste good to you." She agreed.

I sat with her, having a cup of coffee while she ate a cheese sandwich and drank some orange juice. We chatted about the weather, about the changes in the clinic since the last time she had been here some years before, and about the long, bumpy taxi ride that had begun her day. I asked why she had taken a taxi, since she lived so far away, and she said that she had no one to drive her. In response to a few questions gently asked, Mrs. Benson revealed the following information about herself.

Her husband had died many years before, and she had no children. She had had one unmarried sister, older than she, but her sister had died a few months before, so she was really alone. Few people visited her in the nursing home because she had "never been one to have much truck with people." She considered herself very independent. "Anyway, you can't depend on human friends the way you can on animal friends." When I asked her whether she had had animal friends, she replied somewhat proudly that at one point she had owned fourteen cats. We talked some about the merits of cats as friends, and she told me at length about one special cat named Baby who had lived to be very old. She started rummaging in her bag, and I asked if I could help her find something. She said she wanted to show me a picture of Baby, which she did.

I remarked, "It must be very difficult to be in a nursing home when you are used to being independent and having lots of cats for company." Her eyes filled with tears, and she said that she hated it. I asked her to tell me a little about the nursing home. She said that it was a terrible place, and she complained about the inadequate care and the poor food. She had lived there about four years. It had not been so bad before her sister had died, but at the present time it was awful. Her sister had been in better health than she, and it was a dreadful shock when she had died. After Mrs. Benson had gone into the nursing home, her sister had stayed on in the house they had shared. She had visited Mrs. Benson and had brought her fruits and cookies. In the months since her sister had died, she had had nothing to look forward to.

I said that it sounded as if she had had a sad time since losing her sister, and I asked why she had felt especially bad today—to make her come all the way to the hospital. She did not know; she just felt sick all over. I said that it seemed to me that holidays were often especially lonesome times when one was not feeling well. Mrs. Benson said that in her family no one took much account of holidays. We were quiet for a moment, and then she went on to tell me that a few days before she had "taken a notion" to go by taxi to look at the house she and her sister had shared. She had found it in terrible disrepair, with broken windows, evidences of vandalism, and bad words painted on the walls. Even the gas pumps looked damaged. "Gas pumps?" I asked.

"Yes. Sister and I ran a gas station for twenty-five years until I had to go to the home four years ago. Then Sister couldn't do it alone."

I said it must have been a very hard experience to see something that had meant so much to her as a home and a business looking so shabby. She replied that it had made her feel sick all over! And besides, when she had gotten back to the nursing home, the director had been furious and had scolded her for going off like that; he had treated her like a bad child. I told her that I thought it was impressive that she had managed to have her own home and her own business for so many years longer than many people manage to work, but I suspected it made it even more painful to try to get used to such a different sort of life. She had never really thought that she would end her days in a nursing home. With some pride, she added that not many women she knew would still be pumping gas at the age of seventy-five. We both laughed.

After some moments of silence I asked: "Mrs. Benson, how can I best help you this evening? I know you came here hoping to stay in the hospital. But the doctor says that it is not possible, and we both have to go along with what he says, even though you are so disappointed." Mrs. Benson looked sad again and said she just did not know. I asked how she had left it with the nursing home, and she said that she had told the director she was leaving for good. I asked whether she would like me to call him and tell him of her predicament: that she had expected to stay in the hospital but was not going to be able to. She said she did not like the place anyway. I said I realized that, but it was an awkward time, since it was the day before a holiday. Maybe the best plan was for her to return to the nursing home that night and then consider other arrangements. She said there was another nursing home in the town that she thought was better and asked whether she could go there. I said I doubted that it would admit patients so late in the day, but I would gladly phone for her. I asked who had helped her get into the home in which she was presently living. She said that her Old Age Assistance worker had made the arrangements.

I said to Mrs. Benson: "How would it be if I call the nursing home director now and tell him what a bad day you have had and that things have not worked out as you had hoped. Then, day after tomorrow, I'll call the Old Age Assistance worker and talk with her about other possibilities." Mrs. Benson said apprehensively that the director would be mad at her. I said that I could help him understand that the doctors had kept her waiting a long time even though she had arrived early and that she could not have anticipated that she would not be admitted.

She agreed to my phoning the nursing home, and I did so from my office. The nursing home director had plenty to say about Mrs. Benson, who was not an easy patient to handle. However, as I listened and voiced some appreciation for the difficulties the nursing home personnel had had with Mrs. Benson, the director became a little pleasanter. He wanted to know when she would be coming, and I told him that it had not yet been worked out, but I would call again when she left. She knew, though she might not be able to admit it, that she had acted impulsively. I asked whether Mrs. Benson could have a little snack when she got home, since she had had a hard day for an elderly person. He said I could tell her they would keep supper warm for her. Somewhat defensively he said that he could not imagine what had gotten into her; everyone had tried hard to make her happy. I told him that although Mrs. Benson had complained about the nursing home, it seemed to me that she was actually sad and angry about all the losses she had suffered: the loss of her sister; the loss of her former home and business; and the loss, or at least the feeling of loss, of all control over her life.

We talked a little about what a remarkable woman Mrs. Benson was, and I felt that the director's attitude toward her had softened.

I returned to Mrs. Benson and reported that she would be welcomed back with a warm supper. She seemed a little less anxious. I then asked her how she thought she could get home. She said she did not have enough money with her to pay for a taxi but that she did have money at the nursing home. I asked, "How would it be if you ride home in an ambulance instead of a bumpy taxi?" She was horrified; she was "not sick enough to need anything like that." I told her I thought she might be more comfortable, since she could lie down for a bit if she wanted to. Furthermore, Medicare would pay most of the cost of an ambulance, but it would not pay for a taxi. She hated to accept charity. I said that Medicare was part of her Social Security, which she had earned during her many years of hard work. She had never thought of it like that. I commented that many people who were used to being self-sufficient and independent forgot that the Social Security and Medicare benefits they received were paid for out of the funds they had put aside during their working years. She brightened a bit and finally said with a chuckle that she would make quite a stir when she got home!

I waited with Mrs. Benson until the ambulance came, and she left in an almost happy frame of mind.

In this interview the worker is called upon to accomplish a goal already determined by her professional colleagues. Although the goal is a reasonable one from the point of view of the hospital, it is totally out of keeping with the patient's perception of herself or her situation. The worker enters an atmosphere characterized by mutual impatience and irritability, and she is viewed by Mrs. Benson as one more opponent.

The worker's first attempt is to acknowledge Mrs. Benson's disappointment. At the same time she has to repeat the fact that Mrs. Benson is not sick enough to be admitted to the hospital. By pursuing this point, the worker is beginning to work with Mrs. Benson where others think she ought to be rather than where she actually is. A real interview begins only when the worker is aware of how the total situation *feels* to the client. With Mrs. Benson's permission, the worker rearranges the setting to reduce stress and to provide an opportunity for them to talk in private.

The worker then abandons entirely the attempt to achieve the goal prescribed. Instead, she turns the interview toward the details of Mrs. Benson's present predicament, using her own knowledge of what a day in a hospital clinic can be like for an elderly person. The chat about neutral subjects of general interest gives Mrs. Benson a chance to reassert her individuality and to relinquish, at least in part, the role of helpless patient and the frightening loss of control that such a role implies. By getting the food for Mrs. Benson, the worker finds a way of giving Mrs. Benson concrete evidence of her concern and her wish to help, which are based on Mrs. Benson's particular needs.

Gradually the worker is able to expand the areas of exploration in a process of getting to know Mrs. Benson, in the service of strengthening the relationship, and in the hope that knowledge so gleaned will clarify the reasons for Mrs. Benson's coming to the hospital on this particular day with the determination to remain. The worker is flexible enough to follow the clues Mrs. Benson gives. She elects to inquire in more detail about Mrs. Benson's animal friends, sensing that this area is a less painful one, and therefore probably a more productive one, for discussion than that of human friends (". . . You can't depend on human friends. . . .").

Although the worker may have wondered whether Mrs.

Benson's protest that she is independent conceals her desire to feel cared for (by being admitted to the hospital), she does not challenge the woman's view of herself but continues her explorations within that context ("It must be very difficult to be in a nursing home when you are used to being independent. . . .").

As Mrs. Benson reveals more of the accumulated losses that have threatened her equilibrium and have forced her to realize how alone and dependent she is, the worker gently gets Mrs. Benson to talk about the specific events that have led her to come to the hospital at this particular time. She ventures to speculate on the unhappiness holidays can bring when one is not feeling well, but when Mrs. Benson denies that holidays are important to her, the worker permits a silence. Mrs. Benson then reveals the incident that apparently pointed up for her the loss of identity and self-esteem she is suffering and that has driven her to seek help at a distant hospital. Mindful of the time-limited service she is able to offer, the worker does not encourage the revelation of more material than she needs to understand Mrs. Benson's anxiety. Rather, she uses the knowledge she has gained to convey both respectful admiration for Mrs. Benson's accomplishments and awareness of the painful changes she has endured in recent years. The worker is careful not to "take sides" by criticizing either Mrs. Benson or the nursing home, and she avoids holding out false hope that Mrs. Benson can return to a former life-style. More by attitude than by words, the worker conveys her confidence in Mrs. Benson's ability to manage. Mrs. Benson's brightened mood and her humorously prideful reflections on her earlier career seem to give evidence that she has caught the worker's feeling of confidence.

At this point in the interview, the worker, having come to some understanding of Mrs. Benson and having established a more comfortable interaction with her, negotiates a shift of focus to the more pressing business at hand. Because she senses the worker's empathy, Mrs. Benson is better able to absorb the reality that she will not be staying in the hospital. The worker is careful to enlist Mrs. Benson's energies and opinions in planning her return to her community, allowing her to feel she has some control over what happens to her. In addition, the worker shifts the focus from the area of feelings to one of practical planning, in order to prevent Mrs. Benson from later worrying that she has said too much. For instance, the worker does not respond directly to Mrs. Benson's rather childlike fear that the nursing home director will be "mad at her" but diverts the conversation to the more impersonal reality of the delay caused by the hospital, which the nursing home personnel would be sure to understand.

In convincing Mrs. Benson to return in an ambulance, the worker adroitly connects Mrs. Benson's pride in her earlier functioning and earning with her entitlement to benefits. Thus, the worker plants the idea that some dependency is safe, proper, and the reward for a life of independence.

Many interviewers have an opportunity at some time to serve in a liaison capacity between the individual client and a community agency or service. This case illustrates the worker's application of some of the principles of client interviewing to a situation involving a colleague. She was aware that the nursing home director undoubtedly was annoyed with Mrs. Benson and that, in addition, he would expect to hear criticisms of the nursing home personnel. The worker was careful to listen to and absorb the complaints about Mrs. Benson and to express her understanding of the problem she presented. Rather than respond to the director's defensiveness, she directed the conversation away from an assignment of fault to one of understanding Mrs. Benson's behavior in the light of her diminished self-esteem.

16

"I Can't Go Through It Alone"

The following interview from a medical social service department illustrates a caseworker's skill in discovering and alleviating anxiety hidden beneath a belligerent exterior.

I was alone in the office when Mrs. Stewart appeared in the doorway and looked around questioningly. In response to my greeting, she inquired whether this was the social service department, and when given an affirmative answer, she walked in and seated herself. She was a nice-looking, brunette young woman, nineteen years old. She seemed ill at ease as she lighted a cigarette and began to smoke vigorously. I asked if there was any way in which I could be of help to her. Mrs. Stewart promptly replied, "Yes, I want to get a statement from the doctor that I'm sick and can't work." Before I had an opportunity to reply, Mrs. Stewart continued: "I guess you wonder what is the matter with me, because I don't look sick. That's the trouble—I'm too darned healthy. Why couldn't it be me instead of some of those other women down there in that clinic that's got a bad heart or something else. I sit down there and think how easy it would be for them to get a statement. They don't need it, but I do, I really do."

As she finished talking, she looked at me and laughed nervously. I said, "Suppose you tell me why you need a statement so much." Mrs. Stewart replied rather aggressively: "Well, I'm not going to tell you all my life history, because you don't need to know it. The fact is that I'm about three months pregnant, and I can't go on working in the factory any more. It makes my back hurt and my heart go fast. I'm not welcome at home since I've stopped working and I'm not bringing home money, so I'm staying with my married sister temporarily. But I can't go on staying there, because her husband hasn't much of a job and she's got a lot of kids. I want that statement so my family will believe I'm sick and let me stay at home without nagging me all the time."

At this point Mrs. Stewart ran her hand through her long hair and then leaned forward with her face in the palm of her hand, thus creating quite a picture of despair. I asked whether she had already spoken to the doctor in the clinic about her desire for a statement. Quite petulantly she replied: "Yes, I told him I wanted it. He said he could give me one saying that I was pregnant, but he wasn't willing to say I was too sick to work. He seemed to think it would be good for me to work for the next six months. Said a lot of pregnant women work up until the last month." Impulsively she leaned over and took hold of my hand. "Can't you see that's not the kind of a statement I want? It wouldn't do the trick. I have to have one that says that I'm sick—awful sick." I said, "I can see that you are pretty desperate all right and that you must be in quite a predicament or you would not want to be sick so badly." At this moment there was an unexpected outburst of tears. Between sobs she managed to say: "I'm in a fix all right. My husband's in the army, and I want to get him out. Oh! I'll just die if we have to be separated." I commented: "No wonder you want him out so badly. It is hard to face your first pregnancy alone."

Mrs. Stewart continued to sob as she said that they had been married in a hurry so he would not be drafted, and then he had to go because the draft board discovered that their marriage took place after his number had been called. She described, a little hysterically, how he had run away without leave one night in order that they might be together and that his commanding officer had let him off easy because he said he could understand how things were. "I guess it was then I got in this shape. We didn't mean to, of course, but we love each other so much, and somehow we didn't think about the chances we were taking." I inquired quietly, "And now that you are pregnant, how do you feel about having a child?" Mrs. Stewart stopped crying abruptly and said: "Oh, sure! I want him a lot. A lot of my girl friends are married and have babies. We'd have been married sooner, only both of us wanted to work and save our money so we could have a kid."

Her enthusiasm waned again, and she tearfully added: "But I can't go through it alone. He'll desert from the army, or I'll do something to make myself awful sick so he'll have to come home." I said, "I doubt whether it will be necessary for you to do either." I then explained the procedure for filing a formal request for discharge with the commanding officer, who in turn would refer the request to the American

"I Can't Go Through It Alone"
173

Red Cross for investigation, who would get in touch with the hospital about a confirmation of pregnancy. After this explanation, Mrs. Stewart was thoughtful for a few seconds, and then she asked quietly, "And suppose—suppose that doesn't work?" I replied, "It will be hard, but I think you can do it." There was a long silence before the patient said: "I see what you mean. You think I can go through with it alone." I nodded and then added, "Yes, there are women who have to do just that." Quite unexpectedly Mrs. Stewart leaned over confidentially and said, "Well, I guess men aren't allowed in the delivery room anyway, are they?" I told her that in this hospital they were not, and we laughed together about the suffering expectant fathers go through during their lonely vigil in hospital waiting rooms. Mrs. Stewart was still smiling as she got up abruptly and said, "Well, I'll tell Jim to speak to his C.O., but if that doesn't work, I guess it's 'chin up' for me."

A little later, I met Mrs. Stewart as she was coming from the obstetrical clinic. I greeted her by inquiring, "Is it still 'chin up'?" To this Mrs. Stewart replied that she had told the doctor she had never felt better and that she was glad she was good and strong and really could go on working if she had to.

Here, as throughout every interview, the worker is confronted by a multitude of possible responses among which to choose. Many of these flash through her mind almost without her being aware of them. Without time for deliberation she selects the one that at the moment seems best to her. Fortunately, as is often the case, any one of a number of possible choices would have been equally reasonable. On the other hand, of course, there are many responses she could have made that, instead of helping, would have blocked, discouraged, inhibited, or frightened her client. The ability to choose the most effective response quickly and surely comes only with practice and training. One helpful way of improving this capacity in ourselves is to study interviews in retrospect—our own and others—and try to imagine and consider the many responses that might have been made.

In this interview we note again the worker's discerning observation. She is immediately aware of signs of tension and disturbance in this otherwise self-sufficient, healthy-appearing young woman of nineteen: smoking vigorously, laughing nervously, and generally responding aggressively. Under the sympathetic recognition of desperation by the worker she breaks down and cries.

The worker's first response is her question as to whether there is any way in which she can be of help. Consider, for instance, what might have been the result if in this situation the worker had felt it necessary, before proceeding, to obtain full application material and had insisted that the client give information. Or suppose she had felt the need of first explaining to the client the function of the social service department. In either case she would have lost the spontaneous response of the client and probably would have diverted her from expressing her real concern. Instead, the worker offers help in a general way and allows the client to follow her own train of thought.

Mrs. Stewart's first statement about wishing she were as sick as the other women at the clinic might well have stimulated the worker to some such thought as: "How silly to want to be sick," or "How unreasonable," or "You ought to be grateful that you are healthy." She recognizes, though, that, although healthy, the woman is disturbed, and her comment, "Suppose you tell me why you need a statement so much," indicates that she can comprehend the possibility

"I Can't Go Through It Alone"
175

that a well person might want to be ill. The client's aggressive reply, "Well, I'm not going to tell you all my life history . . . ," indicates to the worker that the client, though asking for help, wants to keep the reins in her own hands and maintain some independence. It also indicates that she resents the need to ask for help and has a feeling that by doing so she may be putting herself under obligation to the worker.

A perhaps natural but certainly unwise reaction would have been for the worker to respond to Mrs. Stewart's aggressiveness with aggression or argument. She might have thought, at least to herself: "You don't need to have a chip on your shoulder. Who said I was going to probe and force you to tell more than you want to?" Or this thought might have passed through her mind: "How do you expect me to help you if you are so resistive and unwilling to have confidence in me?" The worker, however, does not ask any of these questions. Instead, she observes the young woman's real despair and inquires whether Mrs. Stewart has asked the doctor in the clinic for a statement that she cannot work, as if she has accepted the client's need to be sick as natural and reasonable. This question is for information and also gives the client reassurance that the worker understands that her need for the statement is real.

The worker's understanding of the situation is summed up in her comment, "I can see that you are pretty desperate all right and that you must be in quite a predicament or you would not want to be sick so badly." This positive comment indicates greater acceptance on the part of the worker than would, for instance, the question, "Why do you need to be sick so badly?" The latter might have seemed accusing to the client, since she had just implied that she did not want to be asked questions. The worker's comment constitutes an interpretation; it restates, in more significant form, material the client has already given. Its accuracy is confirmed by the client's ability to reveal how upset she is. Again, the worker's comment, "No wonder you want him out so badly. It is hard to face your first pregnancy alone," reveals to the client the worker's understanding and acceptance that the client's feelings do not seem unreasonable to the worker, even though they may seem so to others. With this much reassurance she is able to let down the barriers of her defensiveness and to tell a great deal about her feelings concerning marriage and pregnancy.

The worker's question as to how Mrs. Stewart feels about having a child serves both to obtain information and, in case the situation was further complicated by fear or by resentment of pregnancy, to give the client an opportunity to express her feelings. Mrs. Stewart's response clears this issue for the worker, who evidently feels convinced from the woman's spontaneous responses that she does want the child.

The woman's threats that her husband will desert or that she will make herself desperately ill are responded to realistically with information the worker has. The worker might well have been thinking to herself, "What a foolish woman," or have been tempted to argue or threaten her with the dire consequences of such a course. Her mere statement, "I doubt whether it will be necessary for you to do either," implies no blame for having considered these alternatives and suggests that the worker realizes the client is so desperate that either of these courses might seem necessary to her.

By this time the client has, even in this short contact, developed enough confidence in the worker so that she believes the worker really wants to help her, is interested in her, and does not feel that she is foolish or unreasonable. Hence, she can now accept what she would have been unable to earlier in the interview, that is, the worker's expression of confidence in her ability to go through the pregnancy alone.

The shift of Mrs. Stewart's attitude from the beginning to the end of the interview is remarkable. We can see that the change is not merely fortuitous, but took place directly as a result of the worker's handling of the situation and her recognition of the forces at work in Mrs. Stewart. Instrumental also was the relationship built up between the two, even though the relationship was established in such a brief span of time. We can understand what happened when we contrast Mrs. Stewart, unhappy and misunderstood at home, left alone by her husband, and rebuffed by her family, with Mrs. Stewart, listened to understandingly and helped sympathetically by the worker.

Again we see how much a human being needs to share his feelings with someone else and to know that there is someone who understands.

17

"There's a Lot of Other Things Too"

The following interview was condensed from the original one, which was recorded in full as part of a research project in a family agency. The sections included here were selected to demonstrate the worker's skill in overcoming an adolescent's distrust and reluctance to talk and in discovering the underlying reasons for behavior that is difficult to understand.

[The Ames family, consisting of the parents and five sons, applied to the family agency for advice on dealing with threats of garnishments that were jeopardizing Mr. Ames's part-time job with a milling company. Both Mr. and Mrs. Ames seemed to be slow-thinking persons who were very worried about their financial problems. They owed several hundred dollars, principally to loan companies and the company credit union. Bankruptcy proceedings would have cost Mr. Ames his job. Temporary financial assistance was given, and Mr. Ames talked with his creditors and arranged an orderly small-payment system in order to keep his accounts in good standing. With reduced payments on bills, some assistance from the agency, and an increase in work hours, Mr. Ames was able to manage better. When Mrs. Ames was no longer so worried about the bills, she began to talk to the worker about other problems.

The parents apparently lacked ability to deal with the problems of the children. When the second oldest boy, Wallace, refused to attend school (although he was within compulsory school age), Mrs. Ames asked the worker to see him because she was baffled by the situation and his behavior. The following excerpts are from the first interview that the caseworker had with Wallace.]

Wallace Ames came to the agency office. He sat down, his eyes cast down toward the floor. He slouched in his chair, and when I said, "Good morning," and that I was glad to see him, he simply nodded his head. I ask him how things had turned out at the university hospital (the boy had been going to the hospital to clear up a skin rash). He grunted but said nothing. There was a pause. I asked whether he had been at the university hospital the day before, and he said, "Yes."

"Well, did you see Dr. Martin?"

"No, he wasn't there."

Another pause. I went and got the letter we had received from the university hospital and handed it to him. He looked it over and said: "I knew it wouldn't do any good to go there; they don't know anything anyhow. They just make you sit around, and after a while some guy tells you that he can't do anything. Then you pay your money—or maybe you pay the fee first—and then you go home. All they want to do is experiment on people over there, and those doctors don't know nothing."

"Well, I wouldn't be too sure about that," I said. "After all, generally doctors at a hospital are trying to help people."

"Yeah? There is nothing that is going to help me, and anyway I don't care whether they do anything for me or not."

"Well, that's all right if you don't want to go over there. I guess that's pretty much up to you. I guess nobody is going to force you to go to the hospital."

At this point Wallace glanced up briefly, then continued gazing at the floor. "You mean you're not going to chase me over there?"

"Yes, that's what I mean. I thought it would make it a little easier for you if the doctor was helping you out in getting this breaking-out business cleared up, but that's up to you whether you want to go there or not."

"Well, having a rash isn't so bad, but there's a lot of other things too."

"Yes, I know there are a lot of things that a fellow has to get figured out and sort of face up to, and I thought maybe you and I could talk things over. Now that is up to you too. If we can be friends and talk together, okay; if not, I won't ask you a lot of questions."

This first section represents the attempt of the worker and Wallace to get together. Each is sounding out the other, the boy suspiciously, the worker sympathetically.

Interviewing an adolescent, as has been demonstrated in chapters ten and fourteen, has special difficulties of its own. Adolescents, even more than most human beings, are torn by confusions and uncertainties. Wallace illustrates some of the outstanding characteristics of adolescents. They are often dominated by the feeling that others do not understand them. They keep their thoughts to themselves, become secretive, exaggerate their secrets, and are convinced that they would be laughed at or misunderstood if they talked. Actually, such an attitude reflects their own inability to understand themselves. They project onto others their own lack of understanding. Further, they are often so successful in withholding their feelings that they do indeed make themselves inscrutable to persons trying to help them. Wallace does both.

In this interview the worker is confronted by a pretty definite determination of the boy not to talk, and there is no simple, easy way to get beyond this point. Sometimes interviews bog down at this stage over the abstract issue: to talk or not to talk. The sooner the interview can be shifted to a discussion of some concrete problem the better. In the beginning, of course, the problem raised must not be such as to arouse the fears of the client, for such fears would simply strengthen his determination to remain silent. It is sometimes difficult to find a relevant subject about which the client can talk freely. Here the interviewer engages in considerable preliminary fencing before succeeding in getting Wallace to talk.

In studying the beginning part of this interview, we are a little handicapped because we do not know exactly what Wallace has been told about coming in for this appointment. If he has had no explanation at all, it would seem natural for the worker to have begun the interview with some such explanation as he gives later. An explanation given at the beginning would have shown Wallace what the worker's attitude would be, so that he might have been able to lower his barriers a little sooner.

The worker does begin with something concrete—Wallace's visit to the hospital. This topic is at least a safe start, serving as a trial balloon to see how the boy will respond. He talks fairly freely about the hospital. The worker's response, "Well, I wouldn't be too sure about that," falls into the boy's argumentative mood, and with hindsight one can see that it might have been better to have accepted more completely how the boy felt about going to the hospital, with some such comment as "Yes, it is pretty discouraging to sit around waiting for doctors and then not have them tell you very much," and then to have followed this comment with the worker's concluding remark that doctors really do want to help people even though it may not always seem that way when they do not provide help immediately.

The worker's comment, "Well, that's all right if you don't want to go over there," surprises Wallace, for it deprives him of one issue he had expected to fight about. The worker's intentions here are obvious: to assure the boy that he will not be forced to do something he does not want to do and that he can make his own decision. In giving clients assurances of this sort, interviewers should be on their guard lest such comments assume too much of a take-it-or-leave-it attitude. "It's all up to you" is sometimes interpreted by the client not as allowing him self-determination, but as reflecting a halfhearted interest on the part of the worker. Here the interviewer's following comment, "I thought it would make it a little easier for you if the doctor was helping you out," expresses his interest and allays the other impression that might have been given by his insistence that it was all up to Wallace. Wallace's remark, "Well, having a rash isn't so bad, but there's a lot of other things too," gives the worker

"There's a Lot of Other Things Too"
183

the clue early in the interview that Wallace does have things on his mind that are troubling him and of which he is aware. The worker's insistence that he is not going to ask a great many questions is good because it allays what is obviously Wallace's anticipatory fear of the procedure.

There was a long pause. Wallace said, "You know my mother and father, don't you?"

"Yes, I do know them."

"Well, the old man, he has been trying to get his bills paid, so we haven't any clothes, and we can't get things like a lot of people can."

"I know your father is, and has been, doing a lot about getting his bills fixed up, and I think he has done a good job of it. So has your mother, and I guess you kids had to pitch in too, and you helped out by being willing to go without a lot of things you might have wanted." Wallace considered for a moment what I had said and responded, "Oh, yeah, well, you don't know the half of it."

There was a pause. I thought he was going to go on and say more, but he did not. I said, "I guess probably I don't know all about it, and I wonder if you want to talk to me about it."

"It wouldn't do any good."

"Maybe it wouldn't and maybe it would; that's up to you."

"I thought you were just going to ask me a lot of questions."

"No," I paused deliberately. "You see, Wallace, I want to be your friend, but I don't want to force myself on you. You and I can talk like one fellow to another. You can say whatever you want to say. I know there are a lot of things that you wonder about, probably a lot of things that make you sort of sore. If you want to talk to me about these things, you go ahead. If you don't want to talk about them, forget it. I understand." He looked at me directly for a moment and then gazed at the floor. There was what seemed to be an almost interminable pause.

Then he said, "Well, there are a lot of things that I don't know if it would do any good to say anything about. You better talk with my mother or somebody else, because what's the use of me talking?" I said, "Look, you're the fellow I'm trying to talk to now. I figure what happens to you and how you feel about things are important, and what you say means just as much as what your mother or your father would say. You seem to me to be pretty angry about something, and you are keeping it inside yourself. Sometimes it does help if we come out and say what's on our mind."

"Yeah, I suppose it does, but what good would it do?"

"Maybe it would help to say it, and then, too, maybe working along together we could figure some of these things out. I understand that you don't want to go back to school, and I guess that that's worrying your mother and father some, and I wonder if you want to talk about that." Another pause.

"It wouldn't do any good."

"Maybe not and then again it might." Wallace looked at me for a moment and then said, "All I want to do is to go to Vocational High School; you don't learn anything at Sheridan."

Wallace now seems to be making a real effort to talk, assigning his difficulty to their poverty. The worker's "I guess you kids had to pitch in too" goes beyond what Wallace has said and expresses the worker's understanding and appreciation of what Wallace has done. Wallace again indicates vaguely to the worker that "you don't know the half of it." The worker agrees that he does not know about it but says, "I wonder if you want to talk to me about it." This comment is met with Wallace's stubborn refusal, "It wouldn't do any good," and again the worker slips into what sounds like an argumentative statement: "Maybe it wouldn't and maybe it would; that's up to you." The worker's tone of voice and facial expression would determine whether it was argumentative. Similarly, the tone of "that's up to you" would indicate to the client whether the worker was giving Wallace freedom of decision or was simply washing his hands of the matter. It would, of course, have been unwise for the worker to make any false promises at this point about his being sure that he could help. The worker's explanation of wanting to be his friend and to "talk like one fellow to another" breaks through some of Wallace's suspicion and leads him to express his desire to go to Vocational High School. This expression represents the first real movement in the interview. Now they can proceed to more specific topics.

He waited for me to make some comment, and I said, "I think it's a good idea if you want to go to Vocational High School. What do you want to take down there?"

A much shorter pause, and then: "Oh, I would like to take woodwork. I got an A in my woodwork at school, and I'd like to take more of that."

"Well, that sounds fine to me. What kind of things did you make?"

"Oh, I made an end table, and I made a floor lamp— no, it was a desk lamp—that had over two hundred pieces of wood in it."

"Well, tell me a little bit about it."

Then, with a sudden freeing of reserve, he talked for

a couple of minutes about some of the details of the construction of his lamp; he ended up by saying, "And I took it home, and my mother thought it was swell, and my father said it was done better than a lot of carpenters that he knew could do."

"Well, that was great, Wallace, and it is fun to build something nice, isn't it?"

"It sure is, but then I guess I'll never get into Vocational High School. Anyhow, you got to have pull to get in there."

"Well, I'm not too sure about having to have pull. Maybe we could work with you and help you get lined up so you could get into that school. One thing I do know is that you have to complete the ninth grade before you can get in now."

"I haven't finished the ninth grade yet, and it doesn't look like I'm going to get to go to school any more unless I can get clothes and stuff, because I ain't going to go to school when I haven't got any clothes to wear."

"Is that the reason you don't want to go back to school now?"

"Well, I haven't got any shoes, and the only pants that I have got are overall pants. I earned the money this summer helping a guy fix the siding on his house. Then I bought some pants for myself, but they're not good enough to go to school. Most of the stuff I have, my older brother wore first and I just don't like it, and I'm not going to go to school." This last statement was made in a defiant tone, and the boy seemed to close up.

He stared off into space, and I noticed that his hands were clenched and that he was red in the face. I said, "I don't blame you for feeling unhappy about that; probably there is some way we can get around it. I think that if you want to go to Vocational bad enough, finishing up your ninth grade is like earning your way to go there, and you do have to have that before you can get in."

"Well, I suppose so. I guess it's just like what happens to a lot of fellows—you know what you want but you can't get it."

"I guess you have to work pretty hard, and I guess all of us have to work pretty hard to get the things we want."

"Sure, that's okay, but it isn't going to do any good for me."

"Well, maybe it can be worked out."

"No, it can't. My dad hasn't got no money, and we can't ask for any help anyplace, and I haven't even got any shoes that will do to wear." At this point he held up his foot and showed me his badly worn shoes. The boy flushed painfully and continued: "It isn't like my dad could help it or anything, 'cause he doesn't lose or throw away his money foolish like a lot of guys do, but he just doesn't make enough so that we can get along right. He promised that he would get me some shoes, but then they started chasing him on the bills. All he could do was to get these shoes fixed, and I can't do anything about it."

I had the feeling that the boy was fairly close to tears at this point and said, "Wallace, I think you're a pretty good boy. You understand what your father is up against."

"Well, it isn't his fault anyhow, and I can't be sore at him, but a guy can't go to school and sit in a room full of girls and everything when he hasn't got the pants that are right and when his face looks all funny and they don't let you take commercial math like you want to."

"What's this business about commercial math?"

"Well, there were some guys in the class that were going to take commercial math. I wanted to take commercial math too, but they said I had to take algebra. They wouldn't let me change and take what I wanted to take. You're supposed to be able to take three subjects that you want, but they would not let me take commercial math."

Wallace spoke with real vehemence, and when I looked questioningly, he went on to say, "I wouldn't have made any trouble if I had been with these other guys, but I don't see why I had to be the one who had to sit in the class with a bunch of girls where you couldn't talk or anything."

"That does seem sort of unfair, but after all, if the school people say something, sometimes you just can't get them to change their minds, and I guess we have to put up with things in order to get it fixed so you can finish the ninth grade and get into Vocational, if that's what you're going to do."

"Yeah, well, it's easy to say that, but just the same I don't like it, and I'm not going back there now."

"That happened last quarter. Do you think the same thing is going to happen again this fall?"

"I don't know. I haven't been there."

"I think that you are saying that you won't go to school on account of the classes they want you to take, but you don't know what the classes are."

Wallace paused, thought that over, and continued: "Maybe you're right there, but there are other things. The doctors, they can't do my face any good, and I still haven't got clothes, and that isn't all there is."

"Do you like the people that you see around school?"

"Oh, most of the boys are all right."

"How do you get along with the teachers?"

"I get along pretty good with most of them."

"Do you get fairly good grades?"

"Sure, when I work I get good grades. I'm as smart as

any of them, but I just don't care about it. They don't teach you anything. You hear it all on the first day, and then it's the same stuff every day."

"Maybe that's so, but somehow I think that by the time you've been attending a class for three or four months you probably do know more than when you went into it."

"Well, maybe that's so, but it doesn't seem like it to me."

"You said that there were some other things too."

"Yeah, but you wouldn't understand them."

"I would try to understand them, and I guess I can't understand them unless you tell me about them, can I?"

"No, you can't."

"As I said to you before, it's up to you, Wallace, how much you want to say and what you want to talk about. Is something still bothering you? I'm not going to ask you a lot more questions. In summing up what we have been talking about here, you figure you haven't got the right kind of clothing to go to school, and I guess probably that you've got some real reason to feel that way. Probably we can work something out with your folks about that. I do think that if you want to go to Vocational High School, we would try to help you in making a plan to get in there. But, of course, it's up to you to get the ninth grade finished. Also, if we can work with you in getting this business at the hospital taken care of, maybe some doctor can do something, but as a matter of fact, as far as I can see; your face looks perfectly okay to me. I think for a guy as grown up as you are that you're making a lot out of something that probably other people don't notice as much as you think they do." With that I picked up the letter from the university hospital and made some motions as though I were going to terminate the interview.

As the interview proceeds to a more realistic discussion of Wallace's difficulties in going to school, he expresses his enthusiasm for woodwork and reveals his desire not to blame his parents. His general suspicion and tendency to displace his difficulties onto others, however, is revealed by his comment, "Anyhow, you got to have pull to get in there." The worker continually reminds Wallace of the reality that he must finish the ninth grade before he can go to Vocational High School. We note the worker's keen observations of Wallace's body tensions—his clenched fists, flushing, and signs of deep emotion. The worker, getting a sense of Wallace's difficulties, is able to respond readily with expressions of sympathy: "I don't blame you for feeling unhappy about that," and "That does seem sort of unfair." Also, his relationship is well enough established so that he can comment appreciatively on Wallace's excuses for his father, "I think you're a pretty good boy," and Wallace in turn easily expresses his dilemma—he's "sore" but he does not know where to place his soreness, because he knows he cannot blame his father.

The interview proceeds with the worker's being able to pick up clues, "What's this business about commercial math?" and at times to secure a response to merely a questioning look. Once again the worker introduces reality by pointing out the things that Wallace can change and those that he cannot: ". . . If the school people say something, sometimes you just can't get them to change their minds. . . ." He points out that Wallace is refusing to go to school on the basis of something that happened the previous year without having found out what courses he might be allowed to take in the current year.

From Wallace's repeated remark, ". . . and that isn't all there is," the worker infers that there is a more basic difficulty that has not yet come to the surface. He attempts to bring it to light by specific questions about the boys at school, the teachers, and Wallace's grades. Because none of these questions leads to what Wallace has obviously been hinting at, the worker decides that he will have to wait until a later interview to discover what it is, and he sums up the interview and moves to terminate it.

Wallace stood up as though he were going to leave, turned around, and said, "There are some other things too. There are some kind of private things that I maybe could tell you about, but I don't know whether I should or not."

"That is up to you. I'd be glad to talk over anything you want to talk about. I know that it is kind of hard to talk, so maybe you'd like to come in sometime again and talk."

Wallace went to the door, turned around, came back, and said, "I sort of thought you were going to ask me a lot of questions and everything, and you didn't do it, and I guess it was all right for me to come in."

"I'm glad you came in, and remember, the door is open if you want to come in again. I guess that I haven't helped you very much, but I can't do much if anybody doesn't want to go along with me, you know."

"Yes, I guess I understand that."

There was an awkward pause for a moment. Wallace went and sat down again and said, "You won't tell my mother about this, because she'd be upset and it would make my dad feel bad if they knew everything I told you."

"Of course I won't tell them all that you say, because there are some things we don't need to talk over with them. There will be some things that I will want to talk with them about."

"It's this way. I am pretty sore at the school, but I still

want to go back there so I can go to Vocational High School, and I am going to go back to school, but that isn't all. I feel so silly when I go to school."

"If it is the clothing matter, I guess we certainly can find some way to solve that problem."

"It isn't just the pants and the shoes and the jacket I haven't got; I got underwear that I can't take my pants off in school, and you'd laugh if I tell you now what it is." His sentence was all jumbled, and the boy was most uncomfortable. I said, "No, I won't laugh, because I know that sometimes there are little things that happen that just hurt like the dickens."

"What I was trying to tell you was that the underwear that I have hasn't any opening in front like a man's underwear has. It's cut-off women's underwear, and when I go to the bathroom, the guys see me and they laugh at me. I have to kind of sneak in, and then when it's gym time, I gotta change my clothes, and. . . ." Wallace was on the verge of tears; in fact, there were tears in his eyes, and he stammered and came to a halt. I said: "Of course that is tough, and I know it. I'm glad you told me about it, because it does help me to understand."

Wallace went on: "And then on my arm sometimes this rash shows, sometimes on my back, and the guys say that I got a dose of something, and that isn't so. Or they make some crack about my old man having had something, and I can't stand it." He began to sob and buried his face in his hands.

"Wallace, that is too bad, and I really am sorry. Now, instead of giving up because some fellows have made cracks, let's figure out what to do so we can get you back where you want to go to school and get you built up so you will have a better chance to go to Vocational."

"There's a Lot of Other Things Too"
193

Wallace wiped his eyes with a quick gesture, and I continued: "You had real courage when you told me about that, and I know it was hard to say these things, but any fellow that's got courage enough to talk that way has the stuff to meet it, that is, to get things figured out and worked on. Now, let's put our heads together and take this thing a step at a time."

The worker has now convinced Wallace of his real desire to help and has given him enough specific suggestions to lead him to feel that perhaps his stubborn feeling that nothing can be done is mistaken. Wallace has been hesitating about revealing the distressing situation that has most inhibited him. His realization that the interview is about to terminate forces him to reveal even this matter. His fear that the worker will laugh at him, as do the boys at school, for wearing women's underwear is allayed, and he is able to reveal his "shame." The worker responds understandingly: ". . . That is too bad, and I really am sorry. Now, instead of giving up because some fellows have made cracks, let's figure out what to do so we can get you back where you want to go to school and get you built up so you will have a better chance to go to Vocational."

The unusual length of time required for this interview seems to have been justified. It would have been unfortunate if the worker had had to end the interview at a given time rather than wait for the final revealing "confession" about the underwear.

18

"Both of You Feel Trapped"

Most of the illustrations of interviewing in earlier chapters have illuminated the interviewer's techniques in talking with one client at a time. But there are many instances in which two or more people come to an interview together. For example, a number of family members may meet with a doctor to discuss the condition of a critically ill relative. Their manifest purpose is to learn about the patient's health. The doctor is likely, however, to go beyond the mere giving of information concerning the patient's physical condition. He will want to assess the capacity of each relative to be supportive of the patient and to further whatever plans need to be made for his later convalescence and recovery. A school principal may want to interview a parent and a child together if the youngster is failing academically or is behaving disruptively in the classroom.

Family caseworkers have always seen more than one family member at a time, particularly in the home. Previously, these contacts were chiefly for the purpose of observing the setting in which family life went on and secondarily to talk with the person (usually the mother) who was the primary client. Although the interview might be conducted in the presence of other family members, it was essentially a one-to-one exchange.

The casework field has been undergoing a major shift toward joint and family interviews in which the worker's aim is more than the deepening of his diagnostic understanding of clients and their problem-producing situations. With increased frequency the caseworker uses the joint or family interview as the primary treatment mode. Such interviews place new demands on the worker. His powers of observation must be expanded to encompass the overt and covert communications of two or more persons simultaneously. And his own responses must be weighed in relation to their possible effect on several persons, each of whom will bring to the interview individual expectations of the help the worker will give and individual needs the worker will be asked to meet.

This interview is the initial one with a couple in their early forties who had been referred to a family service agency for marital counseling. It illustrates an experienced worker's ability to establish a beginning working relationship with two people who are in conflict with each other.

[Mr. Lorman telephoned on February 13 to make an appointment for himself and his wife, saying that their eleven-year-old daughter's school counselor had said he thought they needed marital counseling. I offered him an appointment for the next day and suggested that I get in touch with the school counselor before seeing them.

With Mr. Lorman's consent, I telephoned the school counselor, who confirmed that he had suggested that the Lormans seek help for their marital conflict. He was surprised that this contact with the agency was their first, because he had made the suggestion in December when Beth, who had previously been an excellent sixth-grade student, had begun to fail in several subjects and was daydreaming excessively. He had been talking with Beth regularly, and from what she had said, she had shown some improvement, though he thought she was still under tension because of the home situation.]

Mr. and Mrs. Lorman were prompt for their appointment. Mr. Lorman, a large man, sprawled restlessly in the chair. His facial muscles were taut, and there was an angry expression in his eyes. Mrs. Lorman, a plump, somewhat dowdy woman, appeared less tense than her husband, but her hands moved nervously in her lap.

I asked the Lormans whether they could tell me what seemed to be the trouble. They exchanged angry glances, and Mrs. Lorman launched into a rapid recital. She was "fed up with everything." Her husband was never home. She did not know where he went, but she suspected he was seeing a woman, now a widow, whom they both had known before their marriage. This woman lived in Arbor Heights, fifteen miles from this city. About three months before, Mr. Lorman had left home after they had had a violent quarrel about his not bringing home enough money and about Mrs. Lorman's wanting to go to work. Someone had told her that on one of the days he was away he had been seen in an Arbor Heights restaurant in the company of a woman. When she had faced her husband with what she had heard, he had said only that it "didn't mean anything." Now she had lost faith in him and intended to pay no more attention to him. Instead, she would take care of the children and think about what she wanted out of life.

I noticed, but made no comment, that Mrs. Lorman's light, sarcastic tone of voice was not in keeping with the seriousness of her complaints. I said: "You do seem to have a lot of things troubling you and a lot of complaints about your husband's behavior. Do you think you want to go on with the marriage?" There was a short pause before she replied: "I'm not sure. Maybe yes, and maybe no. It depends on him."

Mr. Lorman had not uttered a word while Mrs. Lorman was talking. Even when I looked expectantly at him, he maintained his silence. In an attempt to draw him into the interview I asked him if he could tell me what he had been hoping we could do when he had called for an appointment. With obvious anger he replied: "How do I know what you can do? I just thought you might help. That's all." I ignored his hostility and remarked that he seemed quite upset. I said I hoped that he could tell me what was causing him to be so unhappy. I wanted to be of help, but I needed to understand how things looked to him too. So far, I had learned only what seemed to be troubling his wife.

Moving about restlessly in his chair and with a deep sigh, Mr. Lorman began to talk. "I can tell you what's wrong! Money is at the bottom of all my troubles." All his working life, since having graduated from high school, he had held two jobs in order to give his family everything they needed. For years he had been head foreman in a small concern manufacturing shoes. He had "started at the bottom" on the assembly line and had worked his way up. "The guys all liked me because I was fair." But with three children to support and with his payments on his house, two cars, and so on, his paycheck could not cover all his expenses. In the evenings and on weekends he worked as a life insurance salesman. He realized that his having a second job had meant that he had had to spend long hours away from home, which his wife did not like, but he added, "She's always had food on the table, all the clothes she needs, and a car to drive so she can do what she wants." Just after Labor Day the previous year (six months earlier), the shoe company had gone out of business. At the time of the interview he had only his evening job, and his income from selling insurance was not too good because of the general recession. Since Bob, the eldest son, had gotten married on Thanksgiving Day, there were just Beth and 15-year-old Jack at home. Mr. Lorman, however, was still paying back a loan he had taken out to put Bob through college.

I referred to Mr. Lorman's statement about money's being at the bottom of all his troubles and commented that, with the loss of his job, he must indeed be under a strain trying to meet so many expenses. "Do you think that you and your wife would not be having trouble getting along with each other if you could find another job?" In a lowered tone of voice that seemed to convey his hurt more than his anger he said, "Yes, I do." Looking directly at Mrs. Lorman, he added: "All she wants from me is the paycheck. Now she's talking about going to work, but I'm not going to let her."

Mrs. Lorman had begun to cry, and I asked Mr. Lorman if he had noticed what his wife was doing. He said that he had noticed, but it did not mean anything because she cried all the time. "Anyway, I'm crying too. You just can't see it." I turned to Mrs. Lorman and asked her gently if she could talk about why she was weeping. Burying her face in her hands, she said, "I just feel so trapped." She would like to go to work, not just for the money, but so that she could have a few friends and have something to think about besides the house and the children. She was very lonely now that Bob had married and was living in another city. And her closest friend, a woman her own age, had died a year before of cancer. Then Mr. Lorman had gone to that "other woman." "Everything is just too much."

I commented that Mrs. Lorman had said she felt trapped. "But from what each of you has been saying, I wonder if perhaps both of you feel trapped but in different ways." Would they both be willing to come back in a week to work on some of their upset feelings and try to understand what was going on between them? They glanced at each other and then said that they would return. At the end of the interview Mr. Lorman's anger seemed to have diminished, and Mrs. Lorman managed a weak smile as they left.

In this interview, in contrast to some of the interviews in other chapters, the worker is not required to offer concrete help with an immediate problem. Although it is not so stated in the record, it is quite likely that Mr. Lorman was aware when he telephoned for an appointment that "marital counseling" is not the kind of service that can be completed in one interview. It is also significant that he asked for an appointment for himself and his wife together—an indication that he thought, at that time at least, that both of them played a part in the conflict. His request for a joint appointment is an important point, because a husband or a wife who is distressed about the marriage frequently seeks help alone in the hope that the worker will become his ally in the conflict and will work to change his partner's attitudes or behavior.

The worker's aim, therefore, was to give both Mr. and Mrs. Lorman an opportunity to present the problem as each of them viewed it and to help them come to a decision about using further professional help. Did they, in fact, feel that they needed and wanted the worker's help, or had they kept the appointment for this interview only because they wanted to placate the school counselor, who had suggested that they needed assistance? The worker used this first contact, therefore, to test the couple's readiness to use help through an ongoing relationship.

An important element in building the Lormans' trust in the worker is her requesting permission to "get in touch with the school counselor" before seeing them. Only in extreme circumstances, when a client's interests must be protected and he is not able to act in his own behalf, is it permissible for a worker to talk to a third party about a client without his express consent.

The call to the school counselor served two useful purposes. First, the counselor was able to confirm that Beth's academic deterioration and her lack of concentration seemed to be linked to the family conflict and that he had suggested to the Lormans that they seek help. Second, the worker was alerted to look for clues as to why the Lormans had waited two months before having come to the agency. Because the delay might prove to be significant in relation to their readiness for help, the worker keeps it in mind as she begins to explore the nature of the conflict and the Lormans' relationship with each other.

In any interview the worker should observe carefully the client's appearance, behavior, and what he is communicating nonverbally. In a joint interview the worker not only has to make these observations of two people simultaneously, but also has to be aware of the quality and quantity of the nonverbal interaction between the two. The worker observes that both Mr. and Mrs. Lorman are under tension. Although

Mrs. Lorman appears less tense than her husband, the worker cannot be sure whether she is indeed less tense or whether her personality is such that she bottles up her feelings and keeps them under tight control. She does observe the "angry glances" they exchange when she asks them to tell her what seems to be the trouble.

It is especially important in a joint interview for the worker not to predetermine which client will be the first to speak. The worker addresses both Mr. and Mrs. Lorman, leaving the way open for them to decide which one will describe their trouble. Since it was Mr. Lorman who telephoned for the appointment, it would have been easy, though a mistake, for the worker to assume that he would serve as the spokesman for both of them. As it was, Mrs. Lorman was the one who responded to the worker's invitation.

Mrs. Lorman, in her "rapid recital" of the many things about her husband's behavior that bother her, recounts the complaints that are uppermost in her mind at the moment —Mr. Lorman's absence from home, her suspicion that he is interested in another woman, and his failure to give her as much money as she feels she needs. Beneath Mrs. Lorman's assertion that she has "lost faith" in her husband and intends in the future to think about her own welfare, one can sense her hurt at being rejected. At the same time the worker notes that Mrs. Lorman's tone of voice does not convey the feeling that she is actually as "fed up with everything" as she claims to be. This discrepancy between the content of her complaints and the manner in which she speaks leads the worker to venture to confront Mrs. Lorman directly by asking, "Do you think you want to go on with the marriage?" The effect of the worker's question on Mrs. Lorman is to help her stop to think for a moment about what she really wants. She is then able to give voice to her uncertainty and ambivalence. The worker probably would not have thought it helpful to Mrs. Lorman to face her with the need to declare her wishes about remaining with her husband if Mrs. Lorman had not already, by her manner of speaking, given evidence of wanting help in improving the marriage rather than wanting to abandon it.

One has the impression that when Mrs. Lorman ended her account of her complaints, Mr. Lorman was acting as if there was nothing more to be said. Even when the worker directs her attention to him and by her behavior invites him to talk, he maintains his silence. By way of acknowledging the importance of his views on the marital conflict, the worker reminds Mr. Lorman that he was the one who requested the appointment. By asking him what he has been hoping the agency can do, the worker conveys respect for Mr. Lorman as an equal partner in the marriage and the worker's belief that Mr. Lorman is equally concerned about finding a way to deal with the conflict. Mr. Lorman then begins to talk, but "with obvious anger." The worker does not counterattack but persists in encouraging Mr. Lorman to reveal his own unhappiness, insisting that she needs to understand how things look to him too.

The worker's expression of concern for Mr. Lorman and his apparent unhappiness enables Mr. Lorman to talk about their difficulties as he sees them. The picture he gives is of a man whose energies have been devoted to earning a living and who now is suffering a loss of status both in the family and as a wage earner because of the economic reverses. As she did with Mrs. Lorman earlier, the worker asks Mr. Lorman a direct question to encourage him to think about what might be at least a partial answer to the marital conflict. ("Do you think that you and your wife would not be having trouble getting along with each other if you could find another job?") When Mr. Lorman answers in the affirmative, the worker notes that he is speaking more out of his hurt than his anger. But the question also pushes Mr. Lorman to look directly at his wife, and he is saying to her, as much as he is to the worker, that he is hurt because Mrs. Lorman seems to want him less because of himself than because he provides her with material things.

The worker then calls Mr. Lorman's attention to his wife's weeping. Her purpose is to promote their interaction with each other rather than solely with the worker—an important element of treatment in any situation involving marital disharmony, since improvement in marital functioning depends upon improvement in the partners' ability to communicate directly with one another. Although Mr. Lorman is able to admit that he did notice what his wife was doing, he is still so caught up in his own pain that he has to devalue its significance. Helping this couple to respond with affectionate concern to each other's signs of unhappiness or anguish will be one of the goals of casework treatment. In the initial interview the worker can do no more than lay the groundwork for what this couple may achieve at some later time.

The next time Mrs. Lorman speaks, encouraged by the worker's gentle question about why she is weeping, her mood has obviously changed. Instead of expressing anger, she is now revealing the hurt feelings that lie beneath the "light, sarcastic" surface. She is able to let the worker (and her husband too) know that she is lonely, that she is suffering from the losses of the past year, and that she feels "trapped."

One of the predominant skills the worker displays in this interview is her choosing not to focus on the details of each client's complaints but keeping her attention centered on the feelings each is expressing. In suggesting that both

Mr. and Mrs. Lorman "feel trapped but in different ways," she uses Mrs. Lorman's own words to convey to them what appears to be the underlying theme of the unhappiness felt by each. Since the specifics of their charges and counter-charges can be worked through in subsequent interviews—if these clients elect to continue—it is less important to examine them now than it is to give voice to the emotional tenor of the interview. If the worker had led them to engage in a fuller discussion of their specific complaints, she would have run the risk of leaving them with the feeling that they were not really understood. If that had happened, it is doubtful that they would have felt it worthwhile to seek further help with their separate but mutual unhappiness.

The interview ends quite abruptly. It is likely, however, that even though the worker gave Mr. and Mrs. Lorman an opportunity to decline further help, she was confident that she had conveyed to both of them her genuine interest in working with them further, her emotional understanding of their pain and unhappiness, and her ability not to take sides in their conflict, but to offer them support in working to-ward a solution to their problem. That she had indeed done so is attested to by their agreement to return the following week to begin treatment.

Recapitulation

Some recapitulation is now in order. In the light of our examination of the interviews presented and the illustrations they have furnished of our general discussion of salient characteristics of human psychology, we can review and summarize our suggestions on "how to conduct an interview."

BEGINNING

No matter how many questions have to be answered, no matter how much information he wishes to impart, the interviewer should always "begin where the client is." After making a brief introductory statement about the manifest purpose of the interview, it is usually most helpful if he asks a few leading questions that will enable the client to express what is on the "top" of his mind. Of course, the interviewer will have thought over the interview in advance and will know fairly definitely what he wants to obtain from it. But by letting his client talk first, he finds out the client's purpose and is able to pick up many leads for the best way of getting the information needed to help him. He knows his goals, but he will keep his plan of procedure flexible until such leads indicate the best course to take.

Somewhere during the interview, and often early, the client should be given a fairly clear idea of what the interviewer and his agency can do to help and of what kind of responsibility the client himself must assume in meeting his problem. Often the matter can be introduced by asking the client, "In what ways did you think we might be of help?" He needs reassurance that he has come to the right place for help, but he should not be overly reassured or led to feel that he is now relieved of all responsibility, that his problem will be "taken care of." Usually a very brief statement of the kind of services the agency tries to render will suffice at first. Later, as the interview proceeds, further explanation of the precise ways in which the agency can help can be given. Often an interviewer finds it useful in closing the interview to review with the client the next steps each has agreed to undertake.

CONTINUING

After the interviewee has told his story in his own way, the interviewer will make use of the clues thus revealed to introduce additional questions and discussion in crucial areas in order to fill out the picture and focus the interview on that territory that promises to be most fruitful for exploration. Expert direction of the interviewer is most called for at this stage. The interviewer must decide on the areas to be explored and the best way of drawing out the client. To elicit information successfully requires the establishment and development of the kind of rapport between the client and the interviewer that will give the client confidence in the interviewer's wish to help and in his having the understanding and knowledge required for effective assistance. Once this confidence has been established, the interviewer can carefully direct the conversation to obtain necessary information about the underlying basic factors of the client's specific problems.

It is not easy to achieve the golden mean of leaving the client free to talk spontaneously and at the same time giving the interview continued direction into fruitful channels. Mere listening and encouragement simply leave the client floundering in the same sea of uncertainty in which he was lost when he applied for help. But overdirection can stifle the interview in its infancy by preventing the salient features of the matter from rising to clear awareness.

Again, it is not easy to achieve the ideal balance between relieving a client of the unbearable burden of what seem to him insurmountable difficulties and leaving him with essential responsibility for working out his own destiny. In the interviews we have considered, even when the client was most in need of help, the worker, though doing enough to make the difficulties seem conquerable, has in each case carefully left responsibility and initiative with the client. It is a temptation to work out a solution in full detail, especially when working with children or old people, but this temptation must be resolutely resisted. It is better to have the client feel that the plan is one he has been instrumental in developing and is carrying out, with help to be sure, but essentially on his own initiative, than to have all the details correct.

CLOSING

In bringing an interview to a close, several things should be kept in mind. It is usually a good plan to end with a recapitulation of "next steps." A tying together of the threads of the interview and a restatement of what interviewer and client are each going to attend to before their next conference are valuable. If possible, a definite next appointment should be made. If the interview has involved considerable expression of emotion, the interviewer can usually avoid an emotional letdown by turning his client's attention to objective factors before closing the interview.

One of the most important skills for an interviewer is a knowledge of his own limitations. To know when to refer a client elsewhere, when to terminate an interview, when to explore an emotional situation, and when to leave some area unexplored requires skill that comes only with practice. It is a help to remember that an interviewer seldom aims at a complete personality change for his client; his functions are usually much more limited. He must not stop too soon or too late, but at just the right time. And "the right time" varies from person to person. With growing skill in interviewing, the timing is selected with increased ease and confidence. We realize that such skill cannot be acquired simply by reading a book, but a study of the theory of interviewing and thoughtful consideration of it in the light of one's own practice and experiences in interviewing will help a worker to develop his skill and render increasingly valuable service.